CUSTOMER SATISFACTION

CUSTOMER SATISFACTION

How to Maximize, Measure, and Market Your Company's "Ultimate Product"

Mack Hanan • Peter Karp

amacom

American Management Association

This book is available at a special
discount when ordered in bulk quantities.
For information, contact Special Sales Department,
AMACOM, a division of American Management Association,
135 West 50th Street, New York, NY 10020.

Library of Congress Cataloging-in-Publication Data

Hanan, Mack.
    Customer satisfaction.

    Includes index
    1. Customer service.   2. Consumer satisfaction.
I. Karp, Peter.   II. Title.
HF5415.5.H28   1989   658.8'12   88-48026
ISBN 0-8144-5944-7
ISBN·0-8144-7772-0 (pbk.)

First AMACOM paperback edition 1991.

Printing number

10   9   8   7   6   5   4   3   2   1

To John Beard
    Who taught us the paradox that
A poorly managed business
    Finds it easier to satisfy itself
Than to satisfy a customer,
    While a well-managed business
Finds it hard to satisfy a customer
    And is never satisfied itself.

Contents

Preface

This book is written for every manager who serves a customer—or who serves a manager who serves a customer. In other words, this book is for every manager.

If you manage a business, you are responsible for the satisfaction of all its customers. If you manage a business function, you are responsible for the contribution it makes to the satisfaction of all your customers. Even if you never see a customer, customers see you through the contribution you make to their satisfaction.

You may think that you make products, but you really make satisfied customers. You may think that you make sales, but you really make satisfied customers. If your products, your sales, or anything else, for that matter, do not satisfy, you will not be making them for much longer.

If your dollars are on the line because customer dissatisfaction can cut them off or slow them down, it tells you beyond question what you really make.

It is only the beginning to make customers satisfied. You must manage it, measure it, and market it. You must maximize it. You must make it the way of life for your business. This is different from just making it your livelihood. A livelihood is a means to an end. When customer satisfaction is a way of life, it is the end in itself. When everyone who works for you and with you makes customer satisfaction a way of life, it becomes corporate policy.

It takes everyone working together to make customer satisfaction your corporate policy. One dissident, one single deviation, can unmake it. Alone, you may not have the power to mandate satisfaction as corporate policy. But alone, you have more than enough power to end it.

Anyone who does not contribute fully is not working for your customers. In whose employ are such people? If they do not work in your interest, there is only one answer: They are working for your competitors. There is no better way to put you out of business than to erode the satisfaction that your customers hold for you. Anyone who does that is competing against you. The worst case is when the competitor is you yourself.

Introduction

Customer satisfaction is the ultimate objective of every business: not to supply, not to sell, not to service, but to satisfy the needs that drive customers to do business.

The satisfied customer is the true bottom line. If you think of your purpose as being the manufacture of satisfied customers, you will always know where you must take your business. You will know how close you are to getting there. And you will know why you fall short, where you fail, and, consequently, where you are in default of your mission.

When you manufacture a satisfied customer, you make a source of profits for yourself. You make that customer a seller of your products and services, someone who will sell for you by reference. You make him or her a partner who will grow your business. You make the customer a bulwark against the inroads of competition, a bulwark that will refute and refuse your business rivals. You make the one thing you cannot be in business without: a repetitive market.

What does it mean for a customer to be *satisfied*? It may mean that he is satisfied with his purchase. It may mean he is satisfied with the service that attends it or follows it. It may mean he is satisfied with the relationship within which you do business with him. It may mean he is satisfied that the value you have added to his organization or to its operations exceeds the price by a sufficient amount to be a bargain. It may mean any of these things or all of them. But it must mean one thing for certain: He will do business with you again.

The satisfied customer is the repeat customer. He will buy once more. He will buy in volume over time. He will buy at a high margin. He will buy across several lines of your business. He will form the foundation of your demand base, the repeat purchaser who will be one of the 20 percent or so from whom you derive up to 80 percent of your profitable sales volume. He will be a core customer, a major account that will be one of the cornerstones of your market that both provides you with profit and ensures its continuation.

There can be no greater imperative in business, therefore, than to dedicate yourself to the satisfaction of your core customers. It is only they, by their dedication to you, who can guarantee your success.

The 1990s will require a new management dictionary of customer dedication. All the relevant concepts that contribute to satisfaction will have to be redefined in terms of the central concept of *added customer value*:

- A *satisfied customer* is one who receives significant added value from a supplier, not simply added products, services, or systems.
- A *satisfactory supplier* is one who gives significant added value to a customer, not simply added goods or services.

Satisfaction is the value that has been added to the bottom line of the customer. If the customer's bottom line is profits, satisfaction puts more money there. If the bottom line is productivity or a lifestyle value such as comfort or convenience, satisfaction puts more there, too. In return, the satisfied customer will share some of his newly added value with the satisfactory supplier. Both customer and supplier will be enhanced.

Customer satisfaction is the only meaningful competitive advantage. The business with the greatest number of satisfied customers wins. Satisfaction is the transcending benefit, surpassing all others in the value it adds to customer businesses. Simply having the best product—that is, the foremost product benefits—does not suffice, nor does having the best service, the best systems, the best people, the best prices, or, indeed, the best anything. Unless these features can be applied to a customer's business in such a way that *the customer becomes the best*, they by themselves will never yield customer satisfaction.

Satisfaction must become your ultimate product. You must think of it as what you make and what you deliver, install, and maintain. Of all the qualities of a business, the ability to deliver customer satisfaction is the one that is the most necessary to control. The total quality control (TQC) of total customer satisfaction (TCS) must be your overriding mission.

Industry leadership, and with it the ability to control margins at premium rates, depends on the control of "satisfaction quality." In common with internal quality control, TCS takes place in your engineering facilities, on your manufacturing lines, and in your sales and distribution operations. But TCS goes beyond internal quality control (QC). It extends into your customers' businesses, where you must apply the contribution that your internal QC can make to business functions and processes. That is where you make or break satisfaction, for satisfaction is what the customer gets out of dealing with you rather than simply what you put into it.

You should not interpret "satisfied customers" as meaning that *you* are better. Customers are satisfied because you have made *them* better: better at performing the mainstream operations that provide their revenues or better at performing the peripheral operations that generate their costs. What satisfies customers is the improvement they see in themselves, in their capabilities, their productivity, and, ultimately, in their profits. If you can be a source of their satisfaction, they will share it with you in the same ways.

Customer satisfaction is a universal concern. Even the Japanese, who have applied many revisionist strategies to the management of business, have learned that they are susceptible to its requirements. Their education began in 1985, when Japan's second leading car manufacturer, Nissan, began to substitute increased volume rather than customer satisfaction as its prime objectives. Its car lines became stodgy, failing to attract sophisticated young buyers. As inventory rose, dealers cut back prices, even though they lost money on almost every sale. By 1986, only 31 of 254 dealers were making money. Nissan profit margins dropped below Toyota and Honda. Nobody was satisfied.

It is accurate as far as it goes to say that customers are satisfied with suppliers who make money for them instead of costing them money, but this is only a partial truth. Customers are satisfied with suppliers who do two things:

1. Make or save the maximum amount of money for them, more money than they can add to their own businesses themselves or in partnership with competitive suppliers.
2. Cost the minimum amount of money for them (less than competitive suppliers), by minimizing hidden costs, indirect costs, and all expenditures that must be budgeted as unrecoverable costs instead of returnable investments.

In the final analysis, customer satisfaction is measured in dollar signs and not in smiles. The dollar signs of satisfaction are based on reduced customer costs and increased productivity and sales. They reveal themselves as reorders at high margins with low cost of sales. These are the criteria for a satisfied supplier. You get more business. You get it at premium price points. And you get it at a minimal cost.

In these ways, your own profits are improved. This is the ultimate test of satisfying customers. It is also the ultimate reward.

1

Maximizing Customer Satisfaction

Every company in a competitive business can be presumed to generate some level of customer satisfaction. Otherwise, having no satisfied customers, it would have no market. But customer satisfaction is not just something to have, any more than market share is important if it is small or share of a market's mind—the percentage of customers who are aware of a supplier—is valuable if it is in low numbers. Customer satisfaction must be maximized if it is to count for anything as a competitive advantage.

Putting the Pareto Principle to Work

The maximization of customer satisfaction has two attributes: First, every major customer in your core markets

1

must be satisfied to the maximum extent necessary to gain and maintain him as a confirmed partner. Second, as many core customers as possible in major markets must be satisfied to the maximum extent.

These two attributes of customer satisfaction are based on sound marketing principles. You do not have to satisfy everyone. In fact, there are many customers whose satisfaction is irrelevant. But the satisfaction of some customers is so crucial to your success, as well as to your survival, that not only must you satisfy them best; you must satisfy them always.

The Pareto Principle predicts the effect of every business decision. When you apply it to your markets, it tells you that 20 percent or fewer of all your customers account for 80 percent or more of your profitable sales volume. These are your core customers—the heart of your business. If your criteria have been rational, these "20 percenters" will be your national accounts. Their satisfaction is your mission.

These customers will be your most cost-effective source of profits. Every dollar you invest in selling to them will yield the greatest return. It will do this for three reasons: Your cost of sale to a major account is lower, your volume of sales is generally higher, and your margins on those sales is also higher. Why should this be so? Customer satisfaction makes it so. Customers who have been satisfied once anticipate further satisfaction each time they buy. You have a track record of satisfying them. You will therefore be able to condense your sales cycle with those customers. Because they will meet you half way, your cost of selling to them will be lower.

Your customers' satisfaction should cause them to prefer to do business with you rather than with competitive suppliers. The major payoff of customer preference will be in the full margins you will receive as a result of customer perception of the fullness of your value.

The First Group to Be Satisfied:
The "Growings"

The first classification of customers with whom you must achieve total customer satisfaction (TCS) is your current core market. Satisfying these customers will accomplish two essential objectives: It will help you hold on to your privileged status and it will help you expand and extend your privilege.

You need to ask why you will be uniquely favored. The answer is that, from your customer's point of view, he is satisfied with you because you are helping him to grow satisfactorily. The profits he accounts for in your business are derived from the profits you help account for in his business. Through your application expertise, your knowledge of his business, and your product and service systems, you are adding values to his business that reduce his costs or improve his productivity and sales. Doing business with him improves his profits. He can therefore afford to improve yours.

Because your core customers will always be the customers whose profits you are growing, they will be the customers who will grow you. They are your natural growth partners. Their satisfaction is not merely good for your business; it is absolutely necessary. No customer is more deserving of satisfaction than a member of your core market. A national account must always be a customer whose satisfaction comes first.

The downside risk incurred by failure to satisfy a major customer is unaffordable opportunity loss. You lose the opportunity to grow a customer whose business is the type that you can grow best. The converse of that is your loss of someone who has been helping you to grow your own business. Every grower you have is worth his weight in gold. In the short run, he may be virtually irreplaceable. Sometimes, depending on the industry, you will not have the chance to sell him again for as many as five years. As soon as you lose him, your flow of growth profits will be diminished. The opportunity to make future profits with the same customer will also diminish. Your costs of doing business will simultaneously rise as you are forced to invest in added sales costs to replace them. In one fell swoop, you will incur both direct costs and opportunity costs that cannot be made up, at best, until many sales later with a replacement core customer.

Your core customers can be referred to as the *growings*: businesses you are currently helping to grow and whose satisfaction with you is paramount. They are your principal source of current profits. They can also be expected to be your principal source of short-range future profits, so they are doubly valuable. Once you have secured their satisfaction, you must safeguard your long-term future. This will cause you to concentrate on a second group of customers, your *growables*.

The Second Group to Be Satisfied: The "Growables"

A *growable* is a customer who you are not currently growing even though you have the capability to do so. Some of your growables may be established businesses that you have simply not gotten around to, or they may be ones you have avoided because you do not want to confront a competitor's entrenchment. The rest of your growables will be emergent businesses with the kinds of costs in their processes that you can reduce or with the kinds of sales opportunities that you are good at increasing. Growable businesses challenge your ability to spot the future winners among them and become their growth partners early on.

Taken together, your growings and your growables compose your targets for TCS. If you are successful at satisfying them, it will not matter very much whom else you satisfy. If you are unsuccessful, it will not matter very much either.

The Other 80 Percent

What about the remaining 80 percent? To be selective by concentrating on the satisfaction of your growings and growables is one thing, but should you be more than selective? Should you be exclusionary?

Every manager's standards of performance should require the total customer satisfaction of core customers. This will be the wellspring of the manager's business: the 20 percent who account for up to 80 percent of profits. The standard is so imperative that it cannot be violated or ignored. To fulfill it, there is no substitute for market concentration. If dilution is allowed to occur by succumbing to the allure of satisfying "the other 80 percent," the manager's performance will be undermined. No number of satisfied 80 percenters can make up for the cost-effectiveness of profits derived from serving the 20 percenters.

This does not mean that noncore customers should be dissatisfied or deliberately left unsatisfied if it is cost-effective to satisfy them. What it does mean is that corporate policy should not enforce their total satisfaction. Good business practice should ensure a basic level of satisfaction for all customers, but no manager should be diverted from the major task of satisfying the core of his market. It is far too costly and far too ineffective.

Some managers are troubled by a strategy that ignores more than three quarters of their market. They become more concerned for the mass of no-profit, low-profit, and slow-profit contributors than for the core contributors of high profits. Not only do they attempt to satisfy everybody, they attempt to satisfy everybody equally. The typical result is that they lose their heavy-profit customers who need to be satisfied exceptionally. Easy prey to competitors' promises of greater satisfaction, core customers defect. The managers who have dissatisfied them by trying to be all things to all customers then express their own dissatisfaction. "Only the other day," they say about these lost customers, "they were telling us what great guys we were."

The market for TCS for any business is relatively small. This is fortunate, because otherwise it could never be achieved. The small size of the core market makes it feasible to satisfy it. It also makes it imperative: There is no margin for error, because there are no comparable customers to turn to.

Knowing the Customer's Business

What satisfies a business customer? The easy answer is results. But what constitutes results? Results are the customer's profits that are improved when a supplier's products and services are installed in the customer's business operations. Results do not come from a sale, nor do they come from sales-related services. They come from the skill with which a supplier applies his products and services to the functions, operations, and processes of his customers. Satisfaction values are, by and large, applications values.

Becoming an Applications Expert

In order to fully satisfy your customers, you must possess one capability above all others: You must become applications experts in your customers' businesses. You must know *where* to apply your products. You must know *how* to apply them. Most important of all, however, you must know *what dollar values result* when your applications are added to your customers. This is measured in two ways: How many dollars' worth of costs are reduced? How many dollars' worth of revenues are increased? The hallmark of the applications expert is to know the satisfaction value that he represents and to know it in dollar terms.

Customer satisfaction is applications dependent. In the most literal sense of the word, a supplier must *apply* himself to a customer's business in order to create satisfaction. It is the result of the laying on of a supplier's hands to a customer's business functions where the supplier is an expert. At each touch of the supplier's hands, value must be added. The resulting new dollars—not the resulting good feelings, but the hard, bottom-line cash—generate satisfaction.

A supplier's products, promotion, and proposals do not cause satisfaction, they cause costs. Supplier pricing also incurs costs. No customer is ever completely satisfied with a supplier's product (it could always be customized a bit more or its price could always be lower). In order to satisfy themselves about the added costs they have incurred, customers need to see the results of applying products to their operations; they need to see the added values those operations then yield.

Suppliers who court customer satisfaction must know what their products will do when they are applied to a customer function or process. The single most important aspect of what a product will do is the dollar value of the costs it will free up or the dollar value of the productivity or sales it will bring in. *Where satisfaction is concerned, a product is known by the contribution it makes to a business customer's profits.*

The product, in and of itself, is rarely the agent of customer satisfaction. Neither does a product and service system directly result in satisfied customers. Customers are far more likely to attribute their satisfaction to the appliers who generate the new profits that flow from a system, because customers know that it is people, not products, that supply the essential values on which their satisfaction is based.

Product systems produce performance values that can be measured in operating terms: bytes in electronics barrels in oil or brewing. Their appliers produce profit values that can be measured in financial terms: dollars drawn down from a customer's costs or dollars drawn in from a customer's sales.

Your appliers become the crucial factors in customer satisfaction. Your sales representatives, customer service representatives, technical representatives, and systems engineers—whatever you call them—are the men and woman who interface with customers on a daily basis. They sell. They service. They repair and maintain. They upgrade. They measure and monitor results. They anticipate problems as well as solve them. They make opportunities realizable as well as promise them. To do these things with the partnered help of their customers requires more than good intentions or simply being there. It requires inside knowledge about the customer's business functions they affect. This kind of inside knowledge has a name. It is called *expertise*.

Being Process Smart

There is no substitute for expert "process smarts" if you are going to be able to supply satisfaction. To be process smart means to know how a customer's business operates. This is a type of knowledge separate and apart from being "product smart" in how your own products operate. Process smarts means that a supplier's expert knows what a customer's process should look like, sound like, work like, and cost like when it is operating normally. The expert should have a template of these norms in mind, ready to impose it over the customer's process. Where does the process depart from the norm? Is a manufacturing process throwing off too much scrap? It is down for longer periods of time or at more frequent intervals? Does it go off-spec more often? Is it more labor-intensive? Is it less productive per man-hour? Does it maintain excess inventory? Does it use too much energy, have an undue accident rate, or incur unwarranted insurance or security costs?

Does an office communications center occupy too much space? Do its people take too long to communicate with each other? Do some people sit idle while others overwork? Do decisions suffer delay by awaiting support? Does support suffer delay by awaiting information?

Is a laboratory or research and development (R&D) facility laid out ineffectively? Do its people use unnecessary motions, expose themselves or their work to correctable hazards, or occupy time unproductively because work flow is erratic?

Whatever the customer's business and whichever processes you affect, you must be knowledgeable about three things in order to be process smart:

1. *Your customer's process norm*—what its cost and productivity should be when it is operating at minimal cost and maximum productivity.
2. *Your customer's deviation from the norm*—how the process is actually operating in terms of costs or productivity.
3. *Your standard solution*—how to bring the customer's process closer to norm and how much added net value the solution will amount to.

As the customer's applications expert, you must know how much the net added value will contribute to the customer's business. In this way, you will know the satisfaction value you represent, which translates to your worth as a satisfier to your customers. You will have put a dollar value on it, and will not have to wonder if you are satisfying your customer "a lot" or "a little." You will know how much satisfaction you are providing in the same terms that the customer uses to calculate it: dollars of new profits.

With this in mind, you can look at your people through the customer's eyes and see them the same way your customers do when you represent them as applications experts. If your people demonstrate expertise only in your products, in product features and benefits and how they compare with your competitors, they will not qualify as applications experts. They will be seen as suppliers, not appliers. Are they keepers of the industry norms for customer processes? Are they appliers of solutions to bring customer processes more closely in line with their norms? Are they able to demonstrate the added value of their solutions in both operating and financial terms? Can they predict how many dollars their solutions will yield and how soon? Can they fulfill their predictions?

Customers' processes are the cause of their costs and the sources of their earnings. Customers run their processes the best way they can, but they are never satisfied. They constantly look for improvement. Will they look to you? Will they be satisfied when they do? It is obvious that you cannot satisfy them if you make a negative contribution to a process by adding your cost to it when you sell. You cannot satisfy them if your cost exceeds their gain, even if you make a process marginally better. You cannot satisfy them if they examine what you have done to their operations and see only interruption, disruption, and confusion, where before things were at least getting done, however cost-ineffectively. And you cannot satisfy them, either, even if you make an improvement that they believe they could have made themselves or that someone else could have made for the same investment.

If you are going to satisfy your customers, you can take no refuge in simply "being experts." Your competitors may be able to do much of what you do and in much the same way. To satisfy your customers, you must ensure that nobody can do it better.

The Two Basic Types of Customers

Sales transactions take place in two main types of environments:

1. *Business-to-business sales*—where a business supplier sells directly to a business customer. The customer may be an end-user or an intermediary, such as a dealer, distributor, or value-added reseller.
2. *Business-to-consumer sales*—where a business supplier sells directly to an individual consumer. The sale may be made indirectly through a retail channel or directly through telemarketing, mail order, or

personal presentation at a customer's home or place of business.

Business Customers

Business customers live or die on their bottom lines. Profit is the name of their game. To satisfy such customers, you must improve their profit by adding your own value to the values they are able to create without you. No matter what function of their business you sell to, it must result in an improved profit. If you reduce one of their costs of doing business, it must yield an increment in their profits. If you improve their product performance or their market penetration capability so that their revenues increase, it must yield an increment in their profits.

Once you have established yourself as a profit improver, you will be judged satisfactory based on the three specifications of profit improvement: *how sure* the customer can be of improvement, *how much* profit you improve, and *how soon* you will improve it. No matter how much or how soon, any relationship that a customer has with you to improve his profits must be sure. Everything starts from there. Only then do how much and how soon become relevant. The more profit, the sooner you can deliver it, the better—and the higher the level of customer satisfaction you will achieve.

Managers who want to come out of their transactions with satisfied customers start at the very beginning with what they know will be satisfying. They do not start out by saying, "Here is our computer-integrated manufacturing system," when they deal with a customer that needs improved productivity. They learn the added value the customer requires in order to be satisfied with his productivity. How much of a departure is it from his current performance? Knowing that, they can then ask, "What if we can help you come this much closer to your objective— a 10 percent improvement in unit output or a 20 percent reduction in downtime over the next six months; would that be satisfactory? If so, we can work together to see, first of all, if it is feasible, and then how we can make it happen in the most cost-effective way." With this approach, satisfaction becomes engineered into their work together from the inception.

Business customers live in a bipolar world. Every function of their business is either a contributor to costs or a contributor to revenues: a cost center or a revenue center. The sales function is unique—it is both. If a function is a cost center, satisfaction comes from reducing its negative contribution. Conversely, in a profit center satisfaction comes from increasing revenue or from increasing the percentage of profits from each revenue dollar. Your mission can be expressed in these terms: How much cost can you reduce or how much revenue can you increase? How long will it take? How sure can the customer be that it will happen?

These are the terms in which business customers think. To them, you represent either an added cost or added profits. It is always one or the other; there is no in between. If you represent yourself as an added cost, customers will obtain their satisfaction with you by trying to reduce it. They will force down your price. This is the vendor's peril. Such satisfaction is fleeting. It depends on the latest deal, the most recent discount, or the amount of free service. As a result, vendors can never establish a consistently high level of satisfaction with their customers. They can satisfy a customer today or even again tomorrow, but they can never achieve lasting satisfaction.

Everything you do to create lasting satisfaction must be based on continuity. Your relationships with customers must be continuous, not transient from sale to sale. Your knowledge of customers must be continuous, not sporadically contrived from proposal to proposal. Your profit improvement must be continuous, not periodic from implementation to implementation. And the way you position yourself must have continuity as well. You must enter your relationships with customers in a consultative capacity. Whatever you counsel your customers to improve in their operations should have a quantifiable positive impact on their profits.

If you counsel a reduction of scrap in a customer's manufacturing operations, you must quantify its impact on profits. If you counsel an increase in productivity in a customer's office operations, you must quantify its impact on profits. If you counsel a customer to improve product quality, to offer greater convenience to his own customers, or to develop a new product or eliminate an old one, you must translate your words into the numerical language of profits. Otherwise, your counsel will be worthless, since no dollar value can be attributed to it. While your counsel may be sound and your intentions impeccable, you will be committing the most unforgivable error a supplier can commit: selling without knowing your value.

How can a customer be satisfied if he does not know from the outset what value to expect? Suppose you add only a little value. Is that automatically unsatisfactory? Should it have been greater, or is it the norm? He will not know. Suppose you add great value. Is that automatically satisfactory? Could it have been even greater? He will not know. When you ask him if he is satisfied, how can he tell?

Individual Customers

In some industries, individual customers base their satisfaction on the same economic criteria that businesses do. Selling to them is similar to business-to-business selling. Either consumers want their profits improved by personal financial services, or else economic considerations are an important factor in determining which products and services they purchase and use, as in health care, automobiles, or real estate. Even though the customer is a single individual and may be referred to as a consumer, his or her satisfaction with suppliers is largely dependent on reducing costs or increasing earnings. How much, how soon, and how surely you can improve a consumer's personal balance sheet will determine how satisfied he is.

In selling to such customers, the value-to-price relationship of your products or services is paramount. Satisfaction will be determined by the value of the difference between what the customer receives and what he pays to receive it. He will perceive what he pays out as an investment and what he gets back as the return on that investment.

Other individual customers base their satisfaction on less quantified—although not necessarily less quantifiable—criteria. The added value they receive may be in the convenience of doing business or the ease and certainty with which they can obtain redress in the event of problems or in the consistency of a service or the comprehensiveness of service warranties. Some benefits, such as a financing package, may have a direct financial value. Other benefits may have an implied financial value, such as the time value of convenience or the savings from the broad or long-term coverage of a service agreement. Still other benefits may be impossible to assign a dollar value to, or it may be unnecessary to do so. What is it worth to like a product's design, its touch and feel, its look that may impart a sense of prestigious elegance or macho masculinity? These benefits are called intangible because no one can hang a number on them. But they work just the same to create or negate satisfaction.

What satisfies a homeowner about painting the interior of his house? The process may be therapeutic for some owners, but for most it is a grand nuisance—worse, many owners say, than moving to a new house. Quick-drying paints that leave no streaks or brushmarks and that are water soluble can help make painting more satisfactory. Satisfaction from their use comes in two forms. One is that the house appears improved. The other is that the time value of convenience can be quantified. Instead of spending two weekends, for example, only one is required. The second weekend is available for something satisfying. How satisfying is the paint? One weekend's worth.

If your customer's satisfaction comes to depend on such subjective assays made by individual consumers, you will know that you are dealing with commodity products whose performance differences have been neutralized by your competition. Sensory impressions then take over from more objective, demonstrable, and results-oriented reasons for being satisfied. Instead of a single all-powerful reason for high satisfaction, there are usually several factors, each somewhat marginal in itself, that together will add up to satisfaction. This is what makes satisfaction with commodity products appear so fickle. A change in only one component can significantly alter the net outcome. With commodities, satisfaction is apt to be dependent on the weakest part of the buyer-seller transaction.

For this reason, many consumer product categories reveal an absence of differentiation in levels of competitive satisfaction that parallels the lack of product differentiation. It is only natural that buying decisions are based so much on price, which is often the only major difference. Satisfaction in these cases is extremely price sensitive. This is the direct opposite of brand satisfaction, where the combination of high value and high price is much more likely to be associated with, and predictive of, customer satisfaction.

In recognition of this fact, businesses that serve individual customers should try to brand their business as a whole to offset the commodity nature of their products. This can make satisfaction less dependent on a specific product and more reliant on overall corporate repute. If the businesses themselves cannot be differentiated from one another, they will be right back where they started.

Rating the Sales Management

Every dollar that a business invests should have the objective of enhancing customer satisfaction. This is a broader objective than simply making products or sales. It can be thought of as *making satisfied customers who will be the sources of sales*. Sales managers should be graded on how efficient they are in making satisfied customers. This should be their principal standard of performance.

The revenue-to-investment (R/I) ratio is the traditional means of measuring a sales manager's efficiency. It compares the number of dollars of investment required to yield each dollar of revenue. It is supposed to show the manager's skill in allocating resources: How much of a bang does he get for each buck? When his efficiency ratio is known, one sales manager can be compared against other managers. The winner can say, "My R/I is better than yours." But that tells nothing about the manager's ability to make satisfied customers.

Many managers believe that striving for high levels of customer satisfaction will have adverse results on their revenue-to-investment ratio. They are afraid that it will heavy up the investment end by requiring more time, more effort, and more resources on a per-customer basis. When a manager asks, "Who is going to pay for all this?" the answer he gives himself is simple: "I am." A corollary question soon suggests itself: "Isn't it better to keep every customer moderately satisfied than try to make them all very satisfied?"

This is the wrong question. It sets aside the 80-20 rule, forgetting that it is not the satisfaction of every customer that is at issue, but the satisfaction of the premium 20 percent of all customers who account for up to 80 percent or so of profits.

What is required here is not so much increased appropriation of investment funds, but more reallocation of them, taking them away from 80 percent of the company's customers and adding them to improving the satisfaction of the 20 percent. That will not necessarily inflate a manager's investment base, but it should pay extraordinary dividends in improving his revenues. For the first time, he will be concentrating his most productive resources on his most profitable market.

The true significance of investing a sales dollar, and therefore the best measure of its manager's efficiency, is twofold. First, how many new customers does it help win?

This can be called a dollar's *conversion efficiency*. How good is it in converting a prospect into a customer? The second measure is, how many existing customers does it help retain? This can be called a dollar's *retention efficiency*. How good is it in amortizing the original conversion investment over successive sales cycles? These two measurements provide a very good idea of how much *customer satisfaction value* (CSV) a manager can get for every dollar he lays out. This ratio of efficiency can be compared with competitive ratios, both for other managers in the same company and for peers at other companies.

The Customer Satisfaction Index

A formula that can be used for measuring a manager's efficiency in making customer satisfaction is the *customer satisfaction index* (CSI). It requires three steps, illustrated here as a football analogy:

1. Divide a market's contribution of revenue dollars by the conversion dollars invested to earn them. This gives a score for the sales offense. The revenue dollars are the points put on the scoreboard and the conversion dollars are the yards that have to be gained to score those points. When revenue dollars have been divided by conversion dollars, the answer can be multiplied by 100 to get the points per 100 yards gained—or in this case, the revenues from satisfied customers per $100 invested.

2. Divide the revenue dollars lost from dissatisfied customers by the retention dollars invested to save them. This gives a score for the defense. The revenue dollars are the points that competitors have put on the scoreboard against you. The retention dollars are the yards they have forced you to yield. When revenue dollars are divided by retention dollars, the answer can be multiplied by 100 to get the points scored against you per 100 yards given up: the losses from dissatisfied customers per $100 invested.

3. Subtract your defensive score from your offensive score to come up with a customer satisfaction index. The index, as well as the offensive and defensive scores that contribute to it, can help you explore some of the most critical issues in customer satisfaction.

What is the average number of dollars you earn from every satisfied customer you win? What is the average number of dollars you lose from every dissatisfied customer who defects? How do you net out? How do you compare this year with last year? Are you getting better or worse at satisfying customers? Is your competition providing more satisfaction than you are? What is the average mean time between winning a satisfied customer and losing him? Is it getting longer or shorter? Are the reasons the same today that they were a year ago, or are they changing? Are you losing customers to the same competitors, or is that changing too?

Some of the signals that this type of analysis can raise will give you a lot to think about.

Suppose you find that it is costing more to satisfy a new customer today, but you are earning more revenues when you do—yet you are retaining satisfied customers for shorter periods of time. What then?

Or, suppose you find that you are winning fewer new satisfied customers and that your business is increasingly based on established customers (your "installed base"), yet satisfied customers are contributing fewer revenues over time. What then?

The most important discovery for you to think about will be this:

- Who are the managers with the best customer satisfaction index?
- What can you learn from them in order to construct a model satisfaction program?
- How can you use such a program to teach your other managers?
- If you teach enough managers, can you become the

industry's standard for customer satisfaction? If you can, you will possess an unparalleled competitive advantage.

The Folly of Self-Assessment

Managers are frequently asked by their top-level leaders to evaluate themselves as satisfiers of their customers. How do they think they are doing? Factors on a checklist are rated according to a scale of one to five or ten, using attributes and characteristics that most managers seem to accept as relevant, if not determinant. Almost always, generic concepts such as "quality" and "reliability" are included, along with "fair," "helpful and informative," and "ethical." Not surprisingly, managers tend to score themselves as superior in a few factors, excellent to acceptable in most others, and "some room for improvement" in one or two, at the most.

In almost every case, these ratings measure something other than the ability to satisfy customers. They are assessments of how hard and how devotedly a group of managers are working, and how reliable, fair, and helpful they are. The fact that virtually every competitor's managers' in each industry come up with similar results is therefore not surprising. Everybody is working hard and is devoted to the same objectives. The question remains: *"Do customers' assessments agree?"*

If no one knows—and most of the time no one does—then self-assessment becomes an exercise in self-gratification. The one thing that can be said for it is that at least it serves to focus management's attention on customer satisfaction. But, at best, it is a shot in the dark.

The only worthwile assessment is the one that is customer driven. This imposes three requirements on every assessor:

1. Know the customer's checklist of what is important.
2. Know the meaning of each category of satisfaction as the customer defines it.

3. Know the customer's assessment of each of his suppliers in each category on the checklist.

It almost always comes as a revelation when the customer's checklist is compared with a supplier's checklist. Sometimes it is difficult to believe that they do business together. Conversely, it is easy to see why they are not working together as partners and why the customer is so susceptible to dissatisfaction that can lead to switching to a competitor. Suppliers are always perilously close to being told one day "what great guys you were."

Suppliers frequently suffer from ignorance bred by familiarity. "We didn't just get into this business yesterday, you know," they say. "If we don't know how to satisfy our customers by now, we'll never know." Or others say, "We've been around a long time. We must be doing something right." But being around can be a long way from earning maximum profits. What about all the accounts that have been lost, all the orders that were smaller than they could have been, all the margins that had to be discounted, and all the opportunities that no one ever knew about because a customer decided to work with someone else? The cost of these missed chances to sell, were it to be made known or even approximated, would be unaffordable.

What You Don't Know Can Hurt

When a supplier thinks he knows what his customers think, he risks exceeding the law of probability if he is correct; if he is wrong, he risks his customers business. Yet most suppliers unknowingly accept these risks everyday. Even suppliers who know what the risks are may offer a rationale for why they accept them. "What you don't know can't hurt you," some say. Or, "If we really knew what our customers expect, and if they knew we knew, we'd have to do something about it." So it remains easier to go on making assumptions until a customer abruptly, and terminally, makes his expectations known.

The customer's reasons are often revealed in the same traumatic way. Because satisfaction is so prone to being thought of in cosmic concepts, inferred meanings abound. Everyone thinks that he or she knows what "quality" means, for example. And everyone does. The problem is that no two meanings are necessarily the same. There is Rolls-Royce quality and there is Jeep quality. There is quality regardless of price—priceless quality—and there is quality at a price. There is intrinsic quality and perceived quality, and no necessary direct relationship exists between them. There is the quality of a product or service and the quality of the experiences involved in buying it, using it, maintaining it, or trading it in. What, then, does "quality" mean?

Quality is a subjective criterion. Other criteria are, by their very nature, comparative. What does "reliability" mean? Is it reliable in comparison to a customer's ideal? If so, what is the ideal? Is it reliable in comparison to competition? Is it reliable in comparison to the customer's needs? If so, would it therefore be unreliable for a customer with different needs?

The market owns the lexicon of satisfaction. Only customer meanings have validity. In reality, there are no other meanings because it is the customer's definitions that must be met. To be a supplier confers a duty to memorize the customers' dictionary. Otherwise, this is the book that customers will throw at you when the buying comes to an end.

Building In Satisfaction

The commitment to customer satisfaction as your ultimate product must be built into the business mission statement. In fact, *satisfaction must be the mission.* A model statement reads like this:

> The business mission is to create and grow the maximum number of satisfied customers for the company in the most cost-effective manner, thereby maximizing profits.

The same commitment to customer satisfaction must dominate management standards of performance:

> The manager is performing according to acceptable standards when customer satisfaction is maximized in each market from which a major contribution is expected, as evidenced by a high and increasing rate of profit growth.

In both the model mission statement and the standard of performance, the same two attributes of customer satisfaction prevail. It is, first of all, central. Second, it is measured by profits for which it acts as the source.

The single most crucial aspect of customer satisfaction is that it is *the source of profits.* That will come as a surprise to many technology-based businesses whose managers believe that profits flow from their R&D or their engineering or manufacturing. It will also surprise financial services and health care managers who believe that profits come from selling products instead of selling—and satisfying—customers. Surprise will also characterize the reaction of industrial managers who believe that profits come from volume—from gallons, barrels, square feet, tons, and other measures of quantity—and financially trained managers who believe that profits come from consistent cost control. But it will not surprise customers. They know where their profits come from. They do not come from new technologies, which often add only new costs. Nor do they come from buying a supplier's inventory even at a low cost. Nor do they come from controlling costs alone, without the infusion of new revenues.

Because customers know the pivotal value of profits, they are satisfied with nothing else. Because customers know where profits come from, the only way to satisfy them is to work with them in the areas of their business that produce profits. When you focus on key profit producers, you will be working with customers on the high-priority areas to which their resources are already dedicated. These areas will always be found in the major businesses and the principal operations and markets that drive a customer's profits. When you target a customer's high-priority areas, you will never have to search for his "hidden needs" or plead with him to fund your proposals when funds are not available. You will be selling from strength, from your own strength into the strength of your customer's major budgeted needs. In this way, you will be able to maximize your opportunity to satisfy.

Customer satisfaction is not a remedial strategy, a soothing poultice to heal the errors of omission or commission in the way you manage your business. Nor is it a residual measure—the sum total of awareness, attitudes, and acceptance—that remains after day-to-day customer frustrations have been smoothed over by time. It is not something that can be tacked on as a codicil to your normal operations or instituted as an afterthought. It should be installed at the very genesis of a business, as soon as a market need is defined and a product or service is conceptualized for its potential benefit. As a component of the product's manufacturing and marketing—indeed, from its very first developmental model, its "Mark One"—satisfaction must be the starting point where a business begins.

Given this market and what we know about its needs, how can we satisfy it and become its premier satisfier? The answer to this question will describe what a buisness has to be, because everything about its organization and operations needs to be a contributor to its satisfaction of the market.

Businesses whose genesis starts with a product miss out on this centralizing focus for their policies and practices—and, all too often, for their products as well. They build what they make and sell it according to technical specifications. They satisfy standards of engineering performance, not customer satisfaction standards. When they get into their market, they pay the piper by spending time justifying the price of their engineering rather than by celebrating the values of customer satisfaction. The first practice impoverishes them by eroding their margins. The second is the only way they can enrich themselves and their customers alike.

Making Satisfaction Predictable

The thirteen telltale traits of a customer-satisfying business that make satisfaction as predictable as they make dissatisfaction extraordinary are:

1. Customer industry specialization
2. Customer data intensity
3. Key customer concentration
4. Consultative sales strategy
5. Long-term customer partnerships
6. Top management involvement with customer top management
7. R&D immersion in customer data
8. Encouragement of innovative customer relationships
9. Customer-inputted products
10. Comprehensive customer support systems
11. Customer training proficiency
12. Weaselproof warranties
13. Joint customer–supplier planning processes

If you were reconstituting your business, starting it anew from scratch, you could easily ensure that all these traits were built into your organization and operations, especially into the standard practices your managers follow. As established businesses, you must add them to your existing culture. This is easier said than done.

Most established businesses are divisionalized along functional or product lines, not according to customer industry. Their data bases are banks of product and process information, not data bases on customer needs for more satisfying profits. Such businesses vend rather than consult, and the continuity of their relationships is measured by the mean time between requests for proposals. They plan alone on how to penetrate customers rather than planning jointly with customers to create partnerships. As a result, their R&D drives from technology and not customer satisfaction. Their product specifications feature operating performance results rather than a customer's bottom-line profit results. They regard support systems as costs, warranty fulfillment as costs to be avoided, and customer training as a reluctant duty instead of the ultimate insurance policy for guaranteeing satisfaction.

Meeting Customers' Most Important Needs: the "Big Eight"

Across practically all major industries, irrespective of whether a business is selling to other businesses or to individual customers, a small number of factors continually emerge as "musts": needs that must be satisfied if a supplier's TCS score is to be among the highest in its industry. Those factors can be called the Big Eight. Their rank order will vary from industry to industry, customer segment to customer segment, and product to product. But they appear so consistently that they must be accorded recognition above and beyond all others.

To understand the role each factor plays in a supplier's TCS score, it helps to consider that the Big Eight fall into three categories as follows:

Product-related factors
 1. Value-to-price relationship
 2. Product quality
 3. Product benefits and features
 4. Reliability
Service-related factors
 5. Warranty
 6. Response to and remedy of problems

Purchase factors
    7. Sales experience
    8. Convenience of acquisition

Product-Related Factors

Factor #1. The Value-to-Price Relationship The relationship between product value and price is so outstandingly important that it deserves first rank in just about every industry. The *value-to-price relationship* is the central factor in determining customer satisfaction. If the value of what you sell is perceived to exceed the price you ask the customer to pay, the single most important basis for satisfaction is created. Unless value exceeds price, there will be no satisfaction. A market will be satisfied to pay for what it gets—that is, to pay a high price for a high value. But no customer will be satisfied to pay through the nose by putting out more than he gets back, no matter how many other satisfactions he finds in the transaction.

From a supplier's point of view, a price that is supported by a high margin is always the most satisfactory price. From the customer's point of view, high value is the unequivocal prerequisite for satisfaction. Therefore, the most mutually satisfying relationships combine high value at a high price. The key to this ideal relationship—ideal because it satisfies both partners—is always value and never price. Satisfaction originates in value. If you are going to be the standard-bearer of satisfaction for your industry, you must start with the values you intend to supply. Your entire business must be structured around them. It is not enough merely to control the quality of your product or weasel-proof your warranties. Your enterprise as a whole must be organized and operated to satisfy.

Low price by itself satisfies no one. The seller is dissatisfied because he receives low margins, which a high cost of sale will nullify. Customers are dissatisfied because they suspect that a price, once lowered, can be lowered still further or that a competitor may make a better deal. That is why vendors are held in low repute and why they are so often ceaselessly traded off one against the other. No price, no matter how low, is ever "the best price." If it is the best today, it will not be the best tomorrow.

Businesses that sell on price, or that say they sell on performance but nevertheless discount their price, can provide only transient satisfaction. They may make a purchasing agent's day, but they have the wrong concept about what constitutes a bargain. They believe that it depends on low price. In reality, it depends on high value. As long as the value is higher than the price, price can also be high and a bargain is assured.

As a supplier, your transcendent allegiance must be to value. You must not only produce it, promote it, and price it, you must know its worth to your customers. In other words, you must know "the value of your value." Only then will you be able to price it. Unless you price it in relation to its worth, you will be unable to profit fully from it. You will end up giving it away as if it were a commodity, never knowing that you may be the value leader.

"Know your value" must be the watchword for every supplier who seeks satisfaction leadership. He must know at all times how much value he can add to his customers. He must be able to quantify the value he adds so that it can be compared with his price. He must promote his value. And he must identify his value so that it is unmistakably associated with him—branded by him—and him alone.

The central importance of the value-to-price relationship is illustrated by the following scenario:

> A manager who commissioned the purchase of a data processing system from IBM was challenged by his directors. "Don't you know that IBM is the high-priced supplier? And don't you know that IBM is not the technological leader? You paid the highest price for less than the highest performance. Why?"

"I had to", the manager answered.

"You *had* to?" he was asked. "What do you mean, you *had* to?' What did IBM do—did its salespeople come in here and hold a gun to your head?"

"They held something even more persuasive," the manager said. "They held a $15 million return on my investment, starting immediately, achieving full payback in year one and recurring annually through infinity."

The manager's response to the question, "How can you be satisfied buying a high-priced low-tech system?" is simple: "Easily."

IBM knew its value; in this case, the specific value it could add to a multiproduct forecasting and inventory control system. Once the customer was made aware of it and could document the net present value of its amount and cash flow, he was satisfied that IBM's solution, whether technically superior or not, was satisfactory.

IBM has a long history of being sensitive to customer values. From its inception, IBM established an open door policy to provide personal access to its president, Tom Watson. The policy became known as "Mr. Watson's Open Door." BSI and The Wellspring Group have developed a program to allow customers access to the office of any supplier's chief executive through a 24-hour telephone call-in service.

The "electronic open door" is available to all customers. Its phone number is their hot line. A special code is assigned to customers in major accounts—the growings and the growables—to ensure an immediate response. The CEO responds directly, always within five working days, through a return telephone call that is confirmed in writing by follow-up hard copy.

Each month, the issues and concerns that enter through the open door are collected for presentation according to a triage format: what is urgent, what is important, and what is customer-specific or situational and therefore a one-time nonrecurring event. Sorted in this way, the issues are reviewed for solution by a Satisfaction

Review Board. The most important needs of the most important customers become intimately known at the time they occur by the managers who can take care of them. As part of each review, the frequency rate of persistent problems can be charted along with the average reaction times for solving them. Stubborn problems with a high rate of recurrence can be red-flagged for the crash attention of dedicated task teams.

In all business-to-business sales, and in most consumer sales, especially in financial services or products where payout and payback are paramount, value is a dollar-based proposition. It must be expressed in the most relevant terms to its market: net profit dollars and their rate of return; the dollar value of current or future costs avoided, reduced, or eliminated; increased revenue dollars and their profit equivalent; dollars from enhanced productivity; dollars reclaimed from investments or work unnecessarily expended; and time saved or reallocated. In every case, when value is spoken of, it is money that talks.

In by far the majority of sales transactions, nothing has a greater value to customers than money. It is readily quantified. It can immediately be put to work as soon as it is received. No customer can ever have enough of it. And each sum returned can be compared against the amount required to be invested for its achievement, providing a familiar and reliable criterion for decision making.

The value-to-price relationship is the keystone of customer satisfaction because it gives the customer new capital sources to reinvest. Not only is his current wealth increased, but the means to improve future wealth are also at hand. The health of his corporate balance sheet may be at stake. Or, if the customer is an individual, his or her personal estate may be significantly affected. Nothing is more important to either of these two types of customers. Consequently, no one can be more satisfying to them than a supplier who can act as a reliable provider of these values. That means two things. A supplier must be able to deliver improved values. And he must know the cash equivalent of those values to his customers.

Few suppliers know the true value of what they sell. They know what their costs are and they know what their prices are, but they do not know what their customers' business costs are. Few suppliers know the value they can add to customer businesses by reducing those customers' costs. Nor do they know their customers' lines of business and the value they can add by increasing customers' profitability. Because they do not know their own value, suppliers cannot communicate it to their customers. As a result, they cannot charge for it. Those suppliers pay a high price for such ignorance: They leave millions of dollars on the table. Their customers pay a high price, too: They remain poorer, lacking the improved profits they could otherwise have received from their suppliers—profits that could, among other things, fund the next round of business with them.

As soon as a supplier knows the value he represents to his customers, he can communicate it as a return on the investment that a customer makes to secure it. The customer's price acts as the investment. The business they transact is transformed from a buy-sell relationship to one based on return on investment. The essence of their transactions ceases to be based on the exchange of the supplier's products for the customer's cash. Instead, cash alone will be exchanged between them: Cash that is invested is exchanged for cash that is returned. Dollars do the performing instead of products. Each of the two parties knows his dollar value to the other. This kind of knowledge is the driving force of mutually satisfactory partnerships. Where does it come from?

In order to satisfy customers through maximizing, or at least optimizing, the value-to-price relationship of doing business with you, you must know four things:

1. You must know a customer's *current values*. How much does an activity or operation now cost him? How much does he make from it?
2. You must know the *normal value* of the improvements you can make in reducing a customer's current costs or increasing his current earnings.

3. You must know *how much closer* you can bring a customer to your norms from the level of his current costs or earnings.
4. You must know *the resulting added value* to him if you can do this.

Your knowledge of the first item picks out your target. It defines the problem you will set about to solve. The second item provides your standard solutions. They tell you if the customer's problem falls within your capabilities to improve them. The third item sets out your customized solution, based on applying your standard solutions to the customer's specific problem. This tells you if the customer is likely to be someone you can highly satisfy: a "growable." The fourth item gives you the basis for pricing your business with the customer.

This information is crucial to defining your value and relating your price to it. It should be collected about every activity or operation that you affect in the life or business of every customer to whom you are committed to satisfying highly—the major customer segments that compose your core market. You will need a dedicated depository for your knowledge. For this purpose, you will have to organize a key customer data base that will be essentially a problem–solution matrix. Every problem and solution will be quantified on a before-and-after basis. The two principal quantification will always be the same: a customer's current values on the one hand and his future values on the other. The current values will represent the customer's situation *before* doing business with you. The future values will represent the customer's situation *after* working with you. The difference between the two values will reflect the customer's degree of satisfaction with your partnership.

Factor # 2. Product Quality   Quality is an assessment of the general goodness of a product. It is the sum total of all the ingredients or components that compose the product and that contribute to the values it adds.

Factor # 3. Product Benefits and Features   Benefits are the specific user values that enhance a customer's activities or operations. *Features* are the physical ingredients or components that yield the benefits. Benefits and features can be independently satisfactory of each other. One can satisfy while the other does not.

Factor # 4. Reliability   Reliability is the combined effect of product and supplier dependability. It is an amalgam how well a product works in comparison to its promise, and the diligence of the supplier in ensuring the product's performance.

Service-Related Factors

Factor # 5. Warranty   The warranty is the supplier's commitment to stand behind his product and provide satisfaction in case performance departs from promise. It is the insurance policy that documents reliability.

Factor # 6. Response to and Remedy of Problems   Response is the supplier's quickness, appropriateness, and sincerity in preventing or reacting to problems encountered in deriving the benefits or operating and maintaining the features of a product.

Remedy is the supplier's quickness, fairness, and attitude in providing repair or replacement for a nonperforming product, even one that may not be covered in a strict legal interpretation of its warranty.

Purchase Factors

Factor # 7. Sales Experience   Sales experience consists of all interpersonal relationships between supplier and customer that surround a sale. It includes the customer's reactions to the supplier's representatives, as well as the representative's selling strategies, knowledge of the customer's business, ability to partner, promises and proof of values, and commitment to deliver and implement what they sell.

Factor # 8. Convenience of Acquisition   *Convenience* is the ease with which knowledge of the supplier's product, testimony of its cost-effectiveness, and acquisition of the product and its related services can be obtained. Convenience conserves the customer's indirect costs of acquisition and certifies the customer sensitivity of the supplier.

Identifying Industry-Driven Satisfactors

The Big Eight satisfactors are universal. They occur in industry after industry. It is impossible to have a high TCS without scoring high in most or all of them. That is why they should be regarded as "musts": They *must* be satisfied, regardless of the business you are in or who your customers are. If you were founding your business today, those are the objectives you should build it around so that the business would have customer satisfaction engineered into it from inception. If you are reviewing your business, you should make the Big Eight the nucleus of your operation.

Each industry will rank the "must factors" in its own order. Some industries will have a short list made up of a smaller number of absolute musts, such as high value-to-price relationship, reliability, product quality, and benefits and features. If those are not well met, there will be no need to refer to the longer list.

Industries that are capital intensive go through recurrent cycles of liquidity crises when they need to conserve capital resources and maximize their allocation rather than take on new balance-sheet debt. At such times, the convenience of being able to obtain off–balance-sheet financing through a supplier's lease program can assume high priority.

In industries that are prone to product recalls or in

which maintenance after purchase is costly and complicated, the comprehensiveness of a supplier's warranty and the completeness with which it is fulfilled can be paramount.

For original equipment manufacturers, the trinity of reliability, product quality, and service may make up the short list that rates some suppliers as satisfactory but screens out many more. Technical customers may score their suppliers on the quality of training they provide, along with financing ability and warranty. Such service-related and purchase-related satisfactors become disproportionately important when the products of all competitive suppliers are perceived to be undifferentiated commodities.

What are the key satisfactors in your industry? This is the critical question you must ask in order to apply the Big Eight factors to your business. Each industry's list acts to modify the Big Eight, rearranging them in their order of magnitude by elevating some and subordinating others, so that a truly personal industry signature is created. As a result, industries identify themselves by their satisfactor profiles. Serving an industry means knowing and respecting its profile. Expanding into a new industry means first expanding your knowledge to include the satisfactor profile of the customers in it who are new to you. Leaving an industry means that you are no longer willing or cost-effectively able to satisfy its needs.

Now you can see why the often-quoted management belief that a good manager can manage anything is a myth. Unless a manager knows how to satisfy a market—namely, by respecting its satisfactors—he will be unable to manage the sale of anything to it. You can also see why there is such a high rate of failure among new-product businesses, new business ventures, and acquisitions into new technology-based businesses. With no history to guide them, their managers lack knowledge about customers' satisfactors. Unable to serve customers, they disservice them. The markets react with dissatisfaction of their own.

Warning Signs of Dissatisfaction

Customers signal their dissatisfaction early. It is rarely provoked by a competitive supplier. Almost always, you will find that you create your own problems. Even worse, you will tend to overlook the signs that would tell you that your customers are finding your partnership less than satisfying. These signs fall into three main categories:

1. *Slowdown.* Customer approval of your proposals comes slower. Projects that are approved may be stretched out or split up into several successive phases, each of which will require its own approval. The flow of customer data slows down.
2. *Putdown.* Access decreases to upper-level customer managers. Contacts are increasingly shunted to lower functionaries. You can still get "upstairs," but it happens less often and with less reward.
3. *Shutdown.* Plans for future work are foreshortened, becoming progressively shorter term. It becomes difficult to open up discussions of migrations for your current work. The customer prefers to wait and see rather than plan and commit.

These signs are symptoms of a developing dissatisfaction. It is useless, and needlessly antagonistic, to attack them directly. Their cause is the problem. What is the customer dissatisfied about? There can be only two types of causes:

1. You are delivering less than the amount of added values that you have proposed and that the customer has depended on. You are falling short. In turn, this is causing the customer to fall short too.
2. You are delivering the amount of added values that you have proposed, but you are delivering them later than the customer has depended on. Because you are late, the customer's cash flow is late too.

If you can correct the cause, the symptoms of dissatisfaction will disappear.

If you are coming up short, one of two things is wrong. Your original estimates are too high or you are unable to deliver on them. If you are coming in too late, your original estimates are too short or you are unable to deliver on them. If the cause is your inability to deliver, one of two things is probably wrong: You do not know enough about the customer's business or you do not know enough about how to affect it. In the first case, your customer data base is deficient. In the second case, the fault is most likely with your applications skills.

Why "Your Money Back" Is Dissatisfying

The temptation should be avoided to guarantee satisfaction by refunding the customer's money. "Your money back" is not a compelling incentive for any sophisticated customer who knows that payback actually represents a loss of the opportunity to earn a positive return. No customer enters into a supplier relationship to break even. To incur opportunity loss instead of making a gain deprives the customer of a chance to profit. No customer can afford to give away growth opportunities—there are never enough of them and they resist programming. One that is lost can rarely be made up.

There is no alternative to results. Your customers are not in business to "almost" prosper. For you, as well, there is no alternative to helping your customers improve their prosperity. If you fail to do that, two things will surely occur: (1) Your customers will not improve your prosperity in return. (2) They will find a competitor of yours to help them grow. As Whirlpool, the leader in home laundry equipment, has said, "Consumers don't want their money back. They want a product that works."

Giving customers their money back deprives them of the return they should have made on it. How can you avoid dissatisfying them in this critical manner? There are three precautions you can take.

1. *Plan to satisfy your customers in small bites, one bite at a time.* When you limit your objectives this way, you increase your chances for success. You have less data to manage. You have fewer strategies to correlate. You have greater control, with fewer variables to surprise you. The shorter time frame between your start and finish makes it less likely for your planning base to undergo significant alteration or for your assumptions about it to become outmoded.

2. *Make conservative estimates of the amount of value you can add to satisfy your customers and the amount of time it will take you to add it.* It is always more likely that you will add less value than your best-case estimates, not more. It is equally likely that it will take you longer to add your value, not shorter, than you plan. You will not dissatisfy a customer by keeping your estimates conservative and achieving them in full and on time. But you will certainly incur dissatisfaction if you do not.

3. *Monitor your progress in a real-time, on-line basis at periodic intervals while you are in the process of implementing your plan.* You can spot problems as they emerge, not when it is too late. You can apply remedies when there is still time enough for them to work or time to try new ones. You can discover new opportunities, either ones that you have not seen before or newly arisen chances to sell. This will enable you to avoid the twin surprises of added costs or opportunity loss before the time frames of your proposals run out and there is nothing to do but say that you are sorry. Apologizing is the one thing that is worse than offering to give back the customer's money.

A New Look at Quality Control

In order to satisfy customers, two things must be true about your product quality: (1) It must meet the customer's specifications on his must list and (2) it must meet the customer's expectations consistently.

What can happen if you miss out on a must is shown by the chief executive officer whose company lost a major customer to irregular quality. When it was good it was very good. But when it went off specification, it was bad. "They threw twenty-five dragons at us," he said about the customer. "Our people were on call all hours of the day, handled their inventory, made just-in-time delivery dates, . . . everything. We fought off twenty-three of them. I don't think that's too bad." While the supplier was taking pride in his hit ratio, the customer was taking his business elsewhere.

Once satisfactory performance has been established—the product works the way it claims the first time and every time—consistency becomes the key to continuing sales. A product must always perform as expected. This enables customers to specify it, order it, and use it, with confidence that it will do what they require it to do and that there will be no surprises. The twin dimensions of quality are *no surprises* and *utter reliability*.

The object of quality control is controlled expectation. The product must always be the same. If product quality declines and customer expectations are defeated, the impact on sales can be greater than a similar degree of decline in any of the other satisfactors. This is because customers feel cheated of value when their expectations have been betrayed. It is as if their own judgment had been shown to be faulty, not the product or its maker. They see themselves as devalued because their expectation of having value added to them has been frustrated.

Expectation has two main sources. Actual experience with a product itself is one influence on customer expectation. But in many industries, advertising is a far more powerful generator than its product of the benefits a customer comes to anticipate. Advertising reaches more customers and prospects than the product itself and is a factor of major importance in predisposing just about all customers to make their original purchase. Indeed, this is the role of advertising: to create expectations of product performance that the product itself will validate. In this sense, advertising is a rehearsal of purchase that must come before use.

Whenever a product fails to meet the expectations that have been created by its advertising, the funds that have been allocated to the advertising are irrevocably lost. The worst combination is controlled advertising coupled with uncontrolled product quality. The velocity of turnover encouraged by the advertising will leave no time to standardize any inconsistencies in product quality, giving the product a foreshortened life and no chance to return its investment. By accelerating exposure, advertising hastens a market's dissatisfaction.

Controlled quality places a premium on uniformity of performance. The customer's comfort level with his assumptions must not be tampered with. Defects, glitches, and outright failures challenge him to react in ways that are unfamiliar and costly. They take his time, energy, money, and goodwill, rendering his transaction totally unproductive.

Predictability is the essence of all satisfactory business transactions. Customers must know in advance what to expect; otherwise, they cannot proceed. Even if a product's performance is less than the best, missing out on parity as well as superiority, it will still be marketable as long as it meets its customers' "must list." Many customers of par or even inferior products remain stubbornly loyal to them in spite of rival entreaties to switch. "At least," the customers say, "we know what we have." It is controlled quality—not the highest quality perhaps, but quality that is consistent at the highest level of predictability. This is the heart of satisfaction.

2

Managing Customer Satisfaction

How do you manage customer satisfaction as your most important product? By maximizing *added value:* If you serve consumers, you must maximize the value you add to their activities. If you serve business customers, you must maximize the value you add to their businesses.

How can you maximize added value? You must help your customers improve their profits and productivity. This means that you must find ways to lower their costs and raise their income. In turn, this will require you to dedicate every capability of your business to the objective of customer satisfaction.

Is your R&D division developing the technologies whose commercialization will maximize customer satisfaction? Are Engineering and Manufacturing making products that can deliver the maximum number of units of satisfaction as well as the optimal number of units of performance? Is Inventory Management maximizing customer satisfaction? What about Quality Control, lease options to purchase, sales and service strategies?

Sales and service are the "point strategies" for satisfaction. They must reach out and touch the innermost aspects of customer business operations. Sales forces must be trained to penetrate a customer's entire chain of command, partnering at each step of the way to discover profit problems and recommend profit-improvement solutions. Service forces must make similar penetrations. At General Electric (GE), the major appliances division has 2,000 service technicians who make nearly 3 million customer contacts each year. Like Sears, GE services what it sells. It regards its service force as a customer-satisfying strategy and so it grades managers and repair representatives on customer satisfaction rather than on the number of calls they make every day. By mailing out 700,000 response cards to follow up customer repairs, GE develops individual customer satisfaction scores that become the major criterion for determining each servicer's salary and bonuses.

Committing to TCS From the Top Down

Total customer satisfaction (TCS) must originate at the top or it can never become a corporatewide commitment. No sales force can sell satisfaction if its top management does not drive the business from it. No sales support force can act as agents of satisfaction unless its top manager acts as the customers' chief satisfier. No sales policy can be built around satisfaction if top management does not base its business policy on enhancing customer value.

At some companies, managers seem to think it is sufficient to put signs on employees' desks saying, "Customer satisfaction is everybody's business," or "A satisfied customer is our proudest product." But the signs themselves do not satisfy; only people do. The top-down drive that generates the signs is imperative. By itself, though, it is insufficient. Sloganeering about the "what" is useless without specifying the "how." A better blueprint for satisfaction asks, "Did you satisfy a customer today? Did you remind him of the value he is receiving from you? Did you find out if he knows he is getting it? Does he agree that it is the value he needs? If not, you should not be reading this sign. You should be partnering with him right now to give him his full value."

Top-down commitment is easier said than done. In most companies, nothing places customer satisfaction at greater risk than for a top manager to make a high-level "executive sales call." At best, it will be innocuous. Platitudes will be exchanged, the old-boy network will be reinforced, and the two leaders will see each other as "our kind of guy." The worst case occurs when the supplier's chief executive satisfies personal needs—not those of the customer—to "we" orient the dialogue. Have you heard how *we* are looking at the next decade? *We* are developing, *we* are designing, *we* are structuring and restructuring, competing and defeating . . . we, we, we, we all the way home. The customer's purposes remain unexplored and unsatisfied. His patience is tested rather than his profits improved.

Customer sensitivity must be a principal attribute of chief executive officers. Search committees should screen for it. Boards of directors should insist on it. "How sensitive," they must learn to ask, "is our CEO to our customers?" Does he, or she, mechanize them as "technical buyers" or "financial buyers" in the manner of an engineer? Categorize them as "proactives" or "reactives" in the manner of a economist? Dollarize them in the manner of an accountant? Or does the CEO aggrandize customers in the manner of a value-adder who knows that satisfied customers are not simply good for a business—they *are* the business?

TCS must drive from the top down. It must make an impact on every business operation. It must have an effect on products to make sure that they are originating in customer needs to reduce cost and increase productivity and sales. It must have an effect on marketing to make sure that products, promotion, and pricing are being planned to add the greatest value to customers by providing the best solutions to their most important problems.

Customer expectation predicts the first purchase. Customer satisfaction predicts repurchase. It becomes the engine of your business continuity, not just because it forecasts repeat sales but because it enables them to be cost-effective. Acceptance does not have to be won over and over again with each sale. Competitive preference does not to be gained at each phase of the sales cycle. The cycle itself can be telescoped, with your qualifying rounds compressed and attention focused on end results rather than on price and performance. No business can maximize its earnings by starting from scratch with each bid, by walking in cold off the street to make a new pitch every time.

In these ways, the dollar value of customer satisfaction reveals itself. It can account for hundreds of thousands of dollars annually in lowered cost of sales. It can also account for millions of dollars in profitable sales volume that would otherwise never be sold. But its true accounting must be reserved for the value of your business continuity, not just staying in business but growing the business at a high, dependable rate. You must be good managers of your growth. To do so, you must never forget that you are merely caretakers of that growth. Its creators, as you should know, are your satisfied customers.

Planning for Satisfaction

Total customer satisfaction cannot be bought. It must be earned the hard way. It cannot be earned by being Mr. Nice Guy, either by saying "we care" when you do not or by subserviently responding, "What time would you like it to be?" when a customer asks you what time it is. Nor can it be earned by telling jokes, trading gossip, or sweetening the deal with a dash of free services or a dollop of discounted price. For a customer to be satisfied, something of value must be added to his business.

Knowing your value, and knowing that you are really adding it to your customers on a regular basis, is so important that you cannot leave it to chance. Each month, General Motors (GM) compiles a report card on most of its 10,000 car dealers that tells them how satisfied or dissatisfied their customers have been with them. The report grades a dealership's sales approaches, service, and other attributes of a well-run business. Ford, Chrysler, and some of the importers do much the same. In GM's case, its managers have been surveying customer satisfaction since the late 1970s. If a dealership scores consistently low, GM will try to help. If it cannot be helped, GM will ease it out. If a dealer wants a second franchise, the first thing GM looks at are his current satisfaction ratings.

Customer satisfaction the way GM goes about it is a planned process in which the customer is the source. You cannot plan satisfaction alone, in isolation. It must be planned in conjunction with your customers. The question to which the plan should be responsive is not, "How can *we* best satisfy our customers?" but, "How can *you*, the customer, be best satisfied in your operations and activities that we can affect?"

A satisfaction plan cannot impose satisfaction. It cannot persuade a customer that he is satisfied nor can it take the dictatorial approach that says, "You *will* be satisfied." Satisfaction cannot be legislated, only conferred. This means that you must achieve it together with your customers in a spirit of cooperation and collaboration.

Planning for satisfaction is *planning with* your customers, not *planning for* them. Your plan's objectives must be your customers' objectives. Its strategies must be strategies that the customer can harmoniously integrate into his ongoing operations, that fit his management style, and that are acceptable to his people. The way the results of the plan's strategies are measured must make sense to the customer as being fair and valid.

Steering the Plan by Its Objectives

The purpose of the satisfaction plan is to enhance customer satisfaction by a specific, measurable amount within a specific, measurable time in specific aspects of his operations. The plan is steered by its objectives. They pin down what is to be done. The plan's strategies specify how and when the objectives are to be achieved.

Your plan's objectives solely affect your customers' businesses. Its strategies affect both you and your customers, because both of you must jointly agree on them, contribute resources to them, mutually monitor their performance, and migrate their results onto new or additional objectives. Objectives, in short, are of the customer, by the customer, and for the customer. Strategies are mutually created and controlled.

The plan's objectives begin where your customers stand now: at the levels of satisfaction they currently enjoy or the levels of dissatisfaction they currently suffer from, in each key category of their relationships with you. Then the plan must specify where you need to grow in each category, and by when. How much improvement is necessary; how much is achievable on a most-likely-case basis; and how much is bearable in terms of the incremental burdens to be imposed on your human and financial resources.

Your plan should commit you to satisfy one or more of three main types of customer objectives.

1. *Financial objectives.* Customer satisfaction can depend on improving your customer's goals for gross revenues or net earnings, or achieving new goals.

2. *Sales objectives.* Customer satisfaction can depend on improving your customer's achievement of current goals for gross sales volume, share of market, unit margins, turnover rate, cost per sales, or length of the sales cycle, or it can depend on achieving new goals.

3. *Operating Objectives.* Customer satisfaction can depend on improving your customer's achievement of cur-

rent goals for new-product development, the rate of commercialization for new developments, manufacturing productivity, reduction in downtime and scrap rate, safety, inventory control, forecasting dependability, conversion of advertising into sales, or warranty fulfillment rates, or it can depend on the achievement of entirely new goals for growth and diversification.

Specifying the Plan's Strategies

You must be satisfied that your strategies will meet three specifications:

1. They will achieve the desired satisfaction objectives.
2. They represent the most cost-effective way to do so.
3. They threaten no major downside risks.

From your customers' point of view, the strategies in your satisfaction plan must yield the maximum rate of return on their investment with you as their supplier. They will measure their return in units of net dollars. From your own point of view, your strategies must also yield positive returns. Both your revenue-to-investment objectives and your investment-to-profit objectives must be maximized.

Service is often misinterpreted as the key to satisfaction. It is not. Service is a component of satisfaction. Service means on-time delivery, after-sale problem solving, technical support, adequate stocking of field replacement inventory, and training of customer operating people. Satisfaction requires more than service. It is the end-objective of service, just as it is the purpose of sales and every other corporate function. Service alone, no matter how superior, is no guarantee of customer satisfaction. All your customers may be satisfied with your service. That only earns you the right to bring every other strategy up to the same superior standard.

In the traditional sense, strategies are regarded as

methods for penetrating a customer, for entering his business even without his cooperation and for conquering the customer's objections, overcoming buyer resistance, and outfoxing your competition. The strategies of satisfaction are entirely different. They are methods of partnering, not penetrating. Their purpose is mutual long-term satisfaction, not simply today's sale. They seek to bring about a change in the customer's business rather than just a change in the supplier's inventory or market share. When satisfaction strategies work, they work for both partners. Otherwise, they work for neither.

Partnering

Partnering in this way is often referred to as a win–win relationship. In terms of customer satisfaction, what does winning mean? First of all, it means that the customer wins new values through his work with you. This is evidenced to him by new profits, new cost savings, new sales increases, new productivity gains, or other measurable improvements. Second, it means that you win too. You win a satisfied customer. You also win new profits, new sales, and new productivity benefits through longer and larger runs. You keep on winning through new testimonials from your satisfied customers that can help you win other customers who need to be satisfied in similar ways.

Partnering strategies have a significant advantage over penetration strategies because the customer is an active participant in partnering but a defender against penetration. As a participant, the customer is in a position to supply two benefits that are normally denied to penetrators.

1. *The customer can provide a partnered supplier with access to decision-making managers throughout the customer organization.* For the most part, these are line and staff people that a penetrator never gets to see because, in their roles, they do not deal with vendors. Their resources

are directed inward, making them available to their own people and, occasionally, to their customers—but hardly ever to suppliers. They are invaluable as partners, opening up the full operating capabilities of the customer's company to a supplier.

2. *The supplier has access to customer information that is generally held to be proprietary, especially in regard to suppliers.* In order to maximize his satisfaction, the customer knows that he must share internal operating data and external market data with supplier partners. If he does not, he deprives himself of the impact of the total capability of the supplier, who will know neither the current baseline of satisfaction that he must work against nor the changes he is helping to bring about. In business, satisfaction cannot take place in the dark.

In order to be taken seriously as a marketer of satisfaction—the industry standard-bearer, the keeper of the norms—you must position yourself to partner with the customer managers who control, and evaluate, satisfaction. There are two attributes of a partnered positioning that address what these managers look for and react to.

1. *You must be customer-process-smart.* This means that you must know how a customer operates the business processes whose satisfaction you can affect and what the current levels of satisfaction are that you are going to try to improve.

2. *You must be customer-market-smart.* This means that you must know how a customer sells his products or services in the markets where you can affect satisfaction and what the current levels of satisfaction are that you are going to try to improve.

You must become expert in one or both of these categories in order to succeed as a maximizer of customer satisfaction.

If you become expert in satisfying your customers in

the operation of their internal processes, you will be positioned as a source of satisfaction by being a cost-reducer and productivity-improver. Customers will look to you when their satisfaction is impaired by unnecessary costs or insufficient output per dollar of cost. They will call you in, for example, to reduce the cost of a constant level of output or increase the output from a constant cost base. They may also call on you to help them avoid a cost they would otherwise have to incur.

As a result of your positioning, you will tend to be invited to partner largely with new start-up businesses that seek to avoid costs and with mature businesses that must reduce or eliminate cost burdens. You will become known as a satisfier of businesses when they are either young or old.

If, on the other hand, you become expert in satisfying your customers in the operation of their sales and marketing processes, you will be positioned as a source of satisfaction by being a sales developer and productivity-improver of the sales function. Customers will look to you when their satisfaction is impaired by unfulfilled market opportunity, insufficient margins, or insufficient output from their sales representatives. They will call you in to increase the profits from a constant level of sales or increase the level of sales from a constant cost base. They may also call on you to help them increase their competitiveness or defend them from a rival's competitiveness.

As a result of your positioning, you will tend to be invited to partner largely with new start-up businesses and growth businesses that must constantly increase sales and market share. Some mature businesses fighting to increase or defend market share may also call you in. You will become known as a satisfier of growing customers.

Calling the Plays: Strategies for Achieving TCS

If achieving total customer satisfaction is your objective, all of your strategies must be designed to maximize satisfaction in the most cost-effective manner. Every strategy must meet the same criterion: *Does it help maximize customer satisfaction most cost-effectively for the customer and for us?* If the answer is yes, a strategy will be a "go." If not, it is a "no-go."

Maximized satisfaction must be your principal strategic screen. Strategies that pass through it should be put into play as the key elements of your game plans for customers. This way, you will know in advance that every play you call has been prescreened for its ability to contribute to satisfaction.

Just as every strategy has a cost and therefore a price, it must also have a value. The strategies for each customer should have the highest value-to-price ratios. These will be the strategies that can be expected to maximize satisfaction for the customer because they yield the highest return on his investment. They should also yield the maximum satisfaction to you because their value enables them to command the highest prices and thereby maximizes your own profits.

Your playbook of high-satisfaction strategies for each customer acts as your account plan. It says, in effect, that this is the level of satisfaction you want your customer to achieve, here are the areas where you want him to achieve it, and here is the time frame within which it will be achieved. The level of satisfaction will be geared in each case to a specific customer activity or operation whose costs you will commit to reduce or whose revenues you will commit to improve.

For each strategy you call, you must know its objective in terms of what it can contribute toward maximizing satisfaction and when the objective is most likely to be reached. This can be called *high-satisfaction selling*. It meets customer needs. It meets your needs. And it forces your competitors to either play your game or be outmatched. The only way they can combat your contribution to customer satisfaction is by maximizing it even more—in other words, by making your contribution submaximal.

In order to do this, they would have to possess one or both of two capabilities:

1. A superior core customer data base on your customer's current activities and operations, their direct costs, and their opportunity costs; or
2. A superior set of norms to add values to customer activities and operations, based on superior capabilities in reducing customer costs or increasing customer revenues.

These capabilities are the ball game. In every market, there is one winner. He may have a data base that is only at parity with his competitors. Then his norms must be superior. Or he may have the preeminent data base and only parity norms. His customer knowledge will help him apply them more accurately. If he has only one of these capabilities and you have both, he loses. If you have both and no one else does, you win hands down.

What does it mean, in the context of customer satisfaction, to "win?" It means that you win the big ones: the big initial orders with the big margins. It means that you win the big reorders: the follow-ons, the upgrades, and the migrations from your initial sales, also at high margins. It means that while there is room alongside you for a Number Two or a Number Three competitor, they should only be able to pick up the slack that you leave for them. What this means is that *there is really no such thing as Number Two*. The rule may be stated this way: Either make maximum satisfaction or prepare to be minimally satisfied.

Value-to-Price Strategy

The management of customer satisfaction is dependent on managing the relationship between the customer's value and his supplier's price. The relationship must always be managed so that the customer receives a *bar-*

gain—a deal whose value is higher than its price even though its price is also high.

Communicating Value   Customer satisfaction tolerates high-priced bargains because the price, while high in a competitive sense, is actually low *when it is compared with the value it represents.* The difference lies in your choice of comparison. Managing customer satisfaction means relentlessly calculating and communicating your value-to-price relationships with customers. It is up to you to make sure that customers know the value you represent day in and day out, year in and year out, over the course of your work together. It is not enough simply to give value. Nor is it enough for you to know your value. Your customers must be made to know it, too. They must know how much and how soon they will receive it.

Calculating Value   The calculation of your value must precede the calculation of its price. This is because price will be based on value. What is it worth to the customer for you to make the improvements in his activities or operations that you are capable of? That should be the true determinant of price, because it is the true measurement of your value. It is acceptable to the customer to pay for what he gets. It is imperative for you to give him more than he pays for so that he will pay more for it.

How can you calculate your value?

1 *Define what a customer gets from you.* If you say it is a product or a service or a product–service system, your value will be fair market value. It will be pegged somewhere between your cost and competitive prices. Discounting will be the name of your game. But if you say that the value a customer gets from you is dollar value, then you can calculate it in terms of his dollars of reduced costs or increased revenues.

2. *Quantify the new dollar values you offer.* How many dollars of costs will be freed up for a customer to use in new ways? How many dollars of revenues will be brought

in for a customer's growth? How many of these two types of dollar values remain after you subtract the costs of obtaining them? The result will give you the customer's return from the investment he will make with you. You can stop here and base your price or go on to a third step.

3. *Quantify the dollar value to the customer of investing the return you have given him on his original investment.* The result will give you the customer's "return on his return," his profit from second derivative growth. This provides you with another place to stop and base your price. If you do not know the investment opportunity he will choose, you can use annual bank interest as your base. A simplified value calculator along the lines of the model shown in Figure 1 can help you get a sense of the values you are dealing with.

You can gain insight into what your price can be for a business customer by comparing the customer's return on his investment with you to its excess over his hurdle rate.

FIGURE 1.   VALUE CALCULATOR.

1. $ Return to customer (value): $ _____

2. Derived from:

    a. $ Reduction from current cost: _____
    b. $ Increase from current revenues: _____

3. At an investment of: _____

4. Which is paid back by: (Month)_____

                                              or

                                         (Year)_____

5. Yielding a rate of return on investment   ___ %
    $(\frac{R}{I})$ of:

This is the minimum rate of return he will accept on his invested capital, the rate that every investment opportunity must hurdle in order to be acceptable. The higher your value is above the hurdle rate, the higher your price can be because of the greater satisfaction the customer will receive from the cost-effectiveness of your return.

You can use the same method of value-basing your price for an individual customer to whom you sell personal financial services or health care.

Value-Delivering Strategies

In order to maximize the value you deliver, you must manage three strategies exceedingly well:

1. *Product management.* You must correlate product quality with market needs, maintain product reliability, and keep product benefits and features competitive.
2. *Product-related services.* You must provide weasel-proof warranties and guarantees, maintain your products (repairing and replacing them as necessary), offer financing, train customer personnel, and provide technical access when things go wrong.
3. *Purchase management.* You must make the product convenient to learn about and acquire. (Those functions are handled principally by advertising, sales, telemarketing, and distribution.)

Allowing for industry variations, those three strategies are the substance of how most customer satisfaction is generated—or, on the downside, lost. Just by looking at them, it is easy to see why satisfaction is so poorly managed by most businesses. The three strategies are typically independent, lacking not only coordination among them but even internal consistency. Except by happenstance, how can they be managed?

Take product management: Correlating product quality

with market needs is dependent on market research for needs evaluation and the regular translation of findings into product research and development. In how many businesses is there an organized process for bringing the market into corporate decisions on the features and benefits that compose product quality? Then to compound matters, how many of these businesses further translate market-needs research to Engineering and Manufacturing? Yet this is the only one of the three components of product management.

Take product-related services: Surrounding a product with a system of services depends on correlating several functions with product management. In how many businesses are warranties and guarantees regarded as satisfaction strategies as opposed to damage-control instruments devised by the legal department to limit a supplier's liability? In how many businesses are customer financing, training, and technical assistance brought together for planning and implementation purposes as a single package, let alone aligned with product management?

Take sales management: Advertising, sales, and distribution are interrelated marketing functions and should therefore be more amenable to single leadership. But in how many businesses are they more than separate dynasties, each fighting for primacy based on who does what for whom? Should advertising pave the way for sales? Or should it act as a promotional supplement instead of a market pathfinder? Is advertising a cause of sales, or should it be regarded as a result and funded accordingly? In how many businesses is distribution thought of as adding a purchase value to the satisfaction of customers or simply as a cost center, serving as an outlet for sales?

The answers tell the story. If you conceive of customer satisfaction as the resolution of several forces coming together at a single point, the customer, then you must ask who directs them there and who applies them with a single, knowledgeable hand? If no one does these things— if there is no organized process for satisfying customers by the union of the three strategies—then any satisfaction that occurs is more the result of chance than your design.

Implementing Your Satisfaction Strategy

Satisfaction strategy must be managed by a single leader, a director of customer satisfaction, who brings together the individual managers of the three strategies. A model customer satisfaction team, which is an organization of this type, is shown in Figure 2. It works best as a formal organization structure, but it can also operate informally, in the ad hoc manner of a traditional task team.

Getting Started

Many managers languish in commercializing customer satisfaction because they do not know how to begin. Others bias their success from the start because they do not begin correctly.

FIGURE 2. THE CUSTOMER SATISFACTION DIRECTORATE.

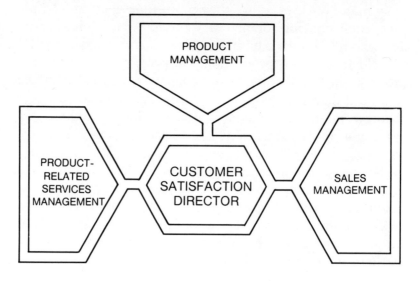

The proper way to begin is with your customers. They must be engaged, but not by you. Through independent third-party research, you must learn two things from them:

1. Their "must list" of where, when, and by how much they need to be satisfied.
2. The comparative scores for you and your competitors in satisfying them.

This is your homework. It will give you a quick fix on where your customers stand in need and where you stand in satisfaction relative to their needs and to the satisfaction being provided by your competitors. Your homework will give you entry to begin the process of becoming the standard of satisfaction for your industry. It will be your calling card to get into the satisfaction business. How can you use it?

The knowledge you gain from your first research provides you with your base line of where you are. From it, you need to create a plan to get where you want to go. Where are you strong? You must plan to stay that way. Where are you weak? You must plan to grow stronger. What are your priorities that are dictated by your customers and your competitors?

Incorporating Customers in the Plan

Your customer satisfaction plan is a two-phase creation. Phase One is yours alone to compile: your objectives and the strategies you best believe will get you there. Phase Two cannot be yours alone. You must bring your customers into your satisfaction plan since it is their satisfaction you are planning. Who knows more about their satisfaction then they do?

By bringing your customers into your plan, your scenario for implementation can begin. To your customers, you can say something like this:

Your mission is the satisfaction of your needs. Otherwise, you cannot maximize your growth. Our growth depends on yours. Only if we help you maximize your growth can we hope to maximize our own. We must therefore go about our business with you in the ways that satisfy you the most. What are they? We need to know.

We have been studying your highest-priority needs and how we currently relate to them. We see where we can improve. We also see where we must stay strong. We have put together a plan to do these things. Before we put it into action, we want you to share in its objectives and the strategies we are considering to achieve them. Have we hit your hot buttons? Are we doing first things first? What have we overlooked? Are there better ways to go about them—ways that may be more effective or less costly, less disruptive, or that will give us both more value?

Please share your best thinking with us because, when we have finished, it will be our mutual plan. To the extent that it is the best plan we can jointly create, each of our businesses will profit. Otherwise, we will incur opportunity costs that will be unsatisfactory to both of us. Each of us will be leaving considerable sums of money on the table. It will symbolize the growth potential that neither of us will ever attain. If we plan properly, however, we will capture it. It will be ours.

Establishing a Directorate of Customer Satisfaction

The customer satisfaction team (Figure 2) crosses several traditional lines of working relationships, bridges coveted turfs, and brings functional managers together in entirely new combinations. The need to challenge tradition like this is proof of how complex customer satisfaction is to manage in businesses organized to make products and services rather than to satisfy customers. It also suggests how different a business would be if it were organized for satisfaction from its inception.

Choosing a Director

The managers of the three satisfaction strategies must themselves be managed. A director must marshall their capabilities in the name of their customers. They and their functions will constitute his directorate. His constituents, as well as theirs, will be your customers. The director will be "their man" inside your business. In turn, he or she must also become "your man" inside your customer businesses. The director must see firsthand their needs, how they go about solving them, and how well you and each of your competitive suppliers score as satisfiers. The director must know your customers' businesses, and your customers must know that the director knows.

The director must be a person of trust. When the director says to the directorate's strategy managers, "We must do thus and so to turn up or turn around our total customer satisfaction rating," they must accept it as gospel. When the director says to the customer's managers, "You and we must do thus and so to maximize your satisfaction with your results from us," they, too, must be accepting. Who inside a typical supplier's business is likely to merit such mutual trust?

You could fool yourself by tossing hats in the ring. The sales manager—he knows our customers. The service manager—he knows them even better. The marketing manager—he used to be both the sales and the service manager. In reality, there is one best answer: *Find someone who knows what it means to be a satisfied customer.* In other words, *find a customer who knows what it means to be satisfied.*

Your director of customer satisfaction should come from a company in the industry you want to satisfy. If there are two or more major industries that you serve, you will need a director for each one. Who else can have the credibility to say internally, "This is what we must do," and be accepted? Who else can have the credibility with customers to say, "This is what we must do," and be accepted?

Customers will only fully accept one of their own. They know that their industry is different in ways that only an insider can know. Conversely, your internal people will never fully accept one of their own. They believe that he knows little more than anyone else about how to satisfy their mutual customers.

The customer satisfaction director must be your ultimate corporate gate-keeper. Everything that passes out the door and impinges on the customers whose satisfaction is the director's responsibility must bear the directorate's imprint. If it fits the customer's criteria for satisfaction—in other words, if it meets the customer's standards of satisfactory performance—then it can be allowed to pass. Otherwise it must not.

Working Together

In keeping the gate with business customers, the director and the three strategy managers will have to partner with customer cost-center managers and managers of the revenue centers that your business affects. With individual customers, such as users of consumer products, partnering will be mediated by market research that defines customer needs and assesses how well they are being fulfilled. The directorate's mission is neither sales nor marketing. It is the centralized management of all of your corporate capabilities that control the company's most precious resource, the satisfaction of its core customers. In short, it is resource management where the resource, in this case, is external to your business and therefore removed from your direct control. It serves an input–output function, bringing in customer needs for your satisfaction and sending out satisfying value that meet the needs. The principle on which it operates is that customers have needs and suppliers must satisfy those needs.

What kind of business is the directorate in? It is in the customer satisfaction business, adding measurable satisfaction values to customer activities and operations. What is its market? It is made up of core customers, the national accounts or heavy users who compose less than 20 percent of all customers but can yield up to 80 percent and more of profits. How is the directorate measured? Its performance is primarily judged by the amount and continuity of core-customer purchase and repurchase at premium margins, the ultimate indicator of maximized satisfaction. A good way to monitor the directorate's performance is to audit a customer's mean time between successive, premium-priced purchases. The shorter the mean time, the higher the satisfaction being created.

No major corporation, which means a company of $100 million or more in annual sales, should be without a directorate to centralize "everybody's business." But what of smaller companies, for whom customer satisfaction is vital in the early years of market entry and crucial in later years for maintaining a competitive position against the giants of the industry?

A company that cannot afford a directorate should form a customer satisfaction panel, composed of a representative sample of the decision makers and users in each industry whose satisfaction is important. On a quarterly basis, for example, the panel can convene to explore opportunities and problems on the basis of improving the mutual profitability of the relationships. Panels can be customer-specific instead of industrywide. In between meetings, or as alternatives to them, correspondence can be exchanged to elicit previews of contemplated policy changes or variations in practice.

Collecting Data

The directorate should have a high *capture ratio* of new customers who are won compared with the number of proposals made to win them. It should have a high *maintenance ratio* of current customers retained compared with the number who defect. It should have a high *upgrade ratio* of additions to your installed base compared with the rate of growth of your new business. It should have a high *reference ratio* of satisfied customers agreeable to testify to their satisfaction compared with the number who refuse. And it should have a high *conversion ratio* of new customers who are persuaded to buy on the basis of testimonials compared with prospects who are converted in any other way.

The directorate must have line operating authority to make enforceable policy. It cannot be an advisory staff whose recommendations can be graciously ignored or allowed to fall between the cracks of the many functional empires it must coordinate. It represents, after all, the heart and soul of your corporate profits. Nothing else your business does is more urgent than creating, maintaining, and growing your core customers' satisfaction.

The work of the directorate will be highly data dependent. It must be your corporate authority on customer satisfaction as well as guardian of the norms of standards of satisfaction for your customers' industries. The acceptance of its satisfaction policy will depend on how well it knows three things:

1. The current state of customer satisfaction in your major accounts, especially your weak areas.
2. Comparative satisfaction levels with your competitors, in your strong and weak areas alike.
3. How to maintain and elevate satisfaction, using the optimal mix of your corporate capabilities.

The first two areas of knowledge must come from ongoing, sophisticated market research. They cannot be left to the cryptic lick-and-a-promise call reports of your sales representatives, grapevine gossip, or the infrequent top-level meetings between your chief executive and the customer's counterpart to ask, "How are we doing? Is there anything else you'd like from us?" No customer will believe a supplier who does not know the customer's business. Nor will the directorate be able to make anything happen internally without the power of validated data.

Line authority will give the directorate its organization power. But only knowledge will give it the power to motivate action.

Customer satisfaction cannot be managed by a supplier alone. Each major customer must be brought into the circuit, his understanding fully engaged, and his cooperation enlisted. He must become acquainted with your objective to maximize his satisfaction, the strategies that you will be committing to achieve it, and the yardsticks the two of you will apply to evaluate your progress. You must partner with him on the mutual nature of your work together—that his satisfaction with you as a profitable source of supply is interdependent with your satisfaction that he is a profitable customer. This will be the basis for your convenant of customer satisfaction.

Our objective [*you can pledge to each core customer*] is to satisfy your requirements at the highest level in the principal aspects of our work with you. Based on our work with you so far, we want to establish baseline ratings of where we stand today in your satisfaction. These ratings will give us our TCS starting points. To remove any possibility of bias on the part of either of us, we will have the evaluations conducted by an independent third party.

We will then compare what we find in your specific case with what we already know—our general norms for satisfaction in each key category of our relationship. Where your satisfaction with us is below our norms, we will work together to raise it. Where we are already above our norms, we will work together to maintain your satisfaction. And where we are right on our norms, we will work to improve them.

We will repeat the independent audit periodically, at a minimum of every four months, to track our progress. We will share the results with you. At the same time, we will be incorporating our experience with you into our general norms so that they will always reflect the maximum levels of satisfactory performance.

This is the way we will work with you for as long as our capabilities are essential to your growth and as long as your satisfaction with them is essential to our own growth—which, of course, will be as long as the two of us are in business."

Spelling out your commitment like this makes it clear to both of you what your business relationship is all about—not an exchange of products for money but maximum mutual satisfaction. What is a core customer to you? Someone to satisfy. Who must you be to him? His preferred satisfier.

Correlating Strategy With Customer Conditions

Five customer conditions will have a continuing influence on the customer satisfaction strategy you devise and how you implement it.

1. Economics
2. Technology
3. Competition
4. Cost-centers and profit centers
5. Life-cycle stages.

Each condition is dynamic, and sometimes two or more of them change at the same time, creating complex problems for both you and your customers. Only one of the conditions is within your control: the situation in a customer's cost centers and lines of business. The other four conditions are far less predictable: the effect of economic influences, the customer's state of the art in technology at any give time, what his competition is up to, and the point he is at—which may not be where he wants to be—in his business life cycle.

Condition #1. Economics

The U.S. economy is disinflating, coming down from its high, pesistent rate of inflationary growth of the 1970s and 1980s to a slower rate. Under disinflation, increased costs can no longer be made up by simply passing them along to customers through higher prices. Now they must be eaten, especially under the price pressures exerted on companies who compete against lower-cost imports or in price-competitive deregulated industries. As a result, the operating strategies of many customers are undergoing radical change. If you are going to satisfy customers in a disinflationary economic environment, you must first recognize what they are doing by themselves to achieve their own satisfactory results. At one and the same time, they are reducing certain operations and increasing others. Customers are *reducing* in ten major areas:

1. Debt as a percentage of total capitalization
2. Capital investments
3. Assets
4. Labor content and labor wage rates
5. Business lines and the size and scope of product lines within them
6. Production and sales cycles
7. Inventory
8. Capacity
9. Quality defects, scrap, and downtime
10. Commodities

How can you create satisfaction with customers who are in a reduction mode? If a customer wants to reduce debt, you may satisfy him by off-balance-sheet financing. If a customer wants to reduce assets, you may satisfy him by helping him buy from you what he must now make for himself. If a customer wants to reduce labor content or shorten his production cycles, you may satisfy him by helping him automate. If a customer wants to reduce inventory, you may satisfy him by installing a just-in-time inventory mix. If a customer wants to reduce defects, scrap, and downtime, you may satisfy him by implementing a quality assurance program.

Simultaneously, customers are *increasing* in ten areas:

1. Productivity
2. Quality
3. Product diversification, emphasizing new products and special proprietary products that can add high value
4. Innovation
5. Worker education
6. Internal controls
7. Vendor controls
8. Margins
9. Specialization
10. Automation

How can you create satisfaction with customers who are increasing these commitments? If a customer wants to increase his productivity, you may satisfy him by automating his office or factory processes. If a customer wants to increase innovation or product diversification, you may satisfy him by providing a data base that matches his market needs with emergent technologies. If a customer wants to increase internal controls, you may satisfy him by providing an internal audit system. If a customer wants to increase his margins, you may satisfy him by supplying innovative components, ingredients, or processes that will reduce his costs or improve his products' sales appeal.

Sometimes a customer's objectives will seem to be mutually exclusive. How can a customer who wants to reduce his capital investment also reduce his labor content without incurring the added capital costs of automation? In this apparent paradox, your solution may come from leasing office and factory automation systems to him rather than selling them outright, thereby keeping his investment at zero.

How can a customer who wants to reduce his business lines also increase his product diversification? Your solution may come from helping him focus on the most profitable lines of his business and developing either high-margin specialty products or integrated families of products within each of them that can serve the same or closely allied markets. In situations like these, your creativity as customer satisfiers will frequently enable you to let your markets have their cake and eat it too.

Condition #2. Technology

In some industries, a customer's satisfaction is dependent on being recognized as the technology leader. Either he is ranked Number One, out on the leading edge, or he drops into the pack of "all others." There is no Number Two. This is frequently the case in science-based businesses, where being the leader can carry a powerful sales edge in the marketplace. Conversely, being hurdled and bypassed by a competitive technology carries an equally powerful but negative influence on the supplier's market position and repute.

A customer who falls behind may never catch up. There is a time lag that sees to that. Even if he does regain parity, the memory of his temporary obsolescence will endure long after he has corrected the fact and he will continue to pay the price in margin and market share.

How can your technical capabilities supplement, complement, aggregate, or rejuvenate the scientific preeminence of a customer's business? If you can act as a strategic ally to his own research and development, or as his creative partner, you can provide satisfaction as a second source. If you can give him a technological difference that his market will perceive as an added value, you will be able to satisfy your customer by virtue of your own scientific leadership.

Condition #3. Competition

Competition is an interruptive influence. It can destabilize the growth of a new customer business, causing it to fall early into maturity. Competition also can destabilize a mature customer business by raising its costs while reducing its revenues and earnings. In both cases, a customer is left with a commodity business whose differentiation will be either temporarily impaired or finally nullified. For these reasons, competition is as dissatisfying as it is destabilizing.

How can you help a customer restabilize a commodity business and thereby provide him with increased satisfaction?

There are two ways to be a satisfactory supplier to a customer besieged by competition. One is to help make him a lower-cost manufacturer and marketer so that he will be able to live with lowered margins. To do this, you must know enough about his operations to know where his key costs tend to cluster and how he can lower them. He will still have a commodity product but it will be more profitable.

The other way to help a customer cope with competition is to restore differentiation to his product in the form of a new or reinvigorated benefit. You may be able to add value through the performance characteristics of your ingredients or components, or by your processes, or by sales and marketing support. If your values can increase demand for your customer's products or give him a justification for maintaining or raising his price, you can help him hold off competition and retain economic health.

Condition #4. Cost Centers and Profit Centers

The monolithic concept of a universal "customer," representing a group of identical individuals all subject to the same strategies for satisfaction, is a conversational convention. No such person exists. The customer who manages a profit center is different from the customer who manages a cost center; it takes different strategies to satisfy each. If customer satisfaction is your primary objective, you must know your manager. Is he a cost-constrainer or a market-penetrator? Does he contribute to corporate profits by reducing and eliminating costs or by increasing sales? Does he believe that it is more important to be the low-cost producer or the high-margin marketer? Does improved productivity mean making more sales calls with the same sales force or spending more time on fewer calls?

Cost-center managers and profit-center managers have dissimilar answers to these and many other questions about what satisfies them. Their points of view are derived from their missions: What do their position descriptions commit them to do and what do their reward systems compensate them for doing?

Satisfying the Cost-Center Manager   There are three levels of satisfaction for the manager of a cost center. The first and lowest level is enabling him to report to his management that he has controlled the rise in his costs to more closely conform with industry norms. If industry costs rose at an average annual rate of 3.5 percent and his costs rose at the same rate, he is in line with his industry.

The second and intermediate level of satisfaction is enabling the manager to report that he has reduced costs below the industry norms. The third and supreme level of satisfaction is enabling the manager to report that he has converted his cost center into a breakeven operation or, better yet, transformed it into a profit center.

How proficient are you as satisfiers of cost-center managers? At what level of their objectives do you satisfy them?

If their costs exceed industry norms, can you help them more closely approximate the norms in their operations that you can affect? By how much? How soon? At what investment and what rate of return? Can you help them do even better than the norms? What is the added value of every dollar of cost that you relieve? What, therefore, is your value as a satisfier?

In order to satisfy customers who manage cost centers, you must be knowledgeable in three areas in which their business interrelates with yours:

1. You must know the cost center's major operations so that you can accurately calculate their current contributions to its cost. This will tell you what its costs *are*.
2. You must know the customer's industry norms for this type of cost center so that you have a standard against which to compare the customer's operations. This will tell you what its costs *should be*.
3. You must know your business well enough to forecast the change that you can introduce into the customer's operations when you try to bring them closer to either the industry norms or your own norms, if they are better.This will tell you what its costs *will be*.

When you sell customer satisfaction to a cost-center manager, you will be selling based on what your norms say his costs should be as contrasted with what they currently are. The difference between the costs that he starts with and what you help him end with will determine your ability to satisfy him.

Satisfying the Profit-Center Manager   There are two levels of satisfaction for the manager of a profit center. The first and lowest level is enabling him to report to his management that he has developed earnings that conform with industry norms for the percentage of profits from sales. If industry profit norms average 7 percent and his rate of profit is the same, he is in line with his industry.

The second and supreme level of satisfaction is enabling the manager to report that his earnings exceed the industry norms or, better yet, lead the industry.

How proficient are you as satisfiers or profit-center managers? At what level of their objectives do you satisfy them?

If their earnings fall below industry norms, can you help them more closely approximate the norms in the product lines and their markets that you can affect? By how much? How soon? At what investment and what rate of return? Can you help them do even better than the norms? What is the added value of every dollar of profits that you increase? What, therefore, is your value as a satisfier?

In order to satisfy customers who manage profit centers, you must be knowledgeable in three areas that interrelate their business with yours:

1. You must know the profit center's markets so that you can accurately calculate their current contributions to earnings. This will tell you what its earnings *are*.
2. You must know the earnings norms for this type of profit center so that you have a standard against which to compare the customer's contributions to earnings. This will tell you what its earnings *should be*.
3. You must know your business well enough to forecast the change that you can introduce into the customer's sales and marketing operations when you try to bring them closer to either the industry norms or your own norms, if they are better. This will tell you what its earnings *will be*.

When you sell customer satisfaction to a profit center manager, you will be selling based on what your norms say his earnings should be as contrasted with what they currently are. The difference between the earnings that he starts with and what you help him end with will determine your ability to satisfy him.

Condition #5. Life-Cycle Stages

In the same sense that there is no universal "customer" as a single entity, there is no monolithic "business." A start-up business is different from the same business after it has made its market entry in regard to what it takes to satisfy its objectives. The same business in growth is still different from entry. In maturity, its needs for satisfaction are different from growth. If customer satisfaction is your primary objective, you must know how to satisfy a customer at each stage of his business cycle.

Is cost control more important then sales? If so, what are the most important costs to be controlled? When does it first become crucial to link the customer's functions of market identification, forecasting and inventory control? At what stage does it make sense to begin proliferation of your original installation? When does a customer start to become dependent on savings as a major source of internal funds?

Customer businesses in the growth stages and mature businesses have dissimilar answers to these and many other questions about what satisfies them. Their points of view are derived from their life-cycle positions: What does their position require them to emphasize if they are going to grow or survive?

In the start-up phase, a customer needs to satisfy the requirements to identify his core market, forecast its demand and drive his inventory from the forecast, ensure productivity, and maintain quality. Upon entry, he requires cash flow from sales. As the business grows, his needs for sales, accurate forecasting, and inventory control become acute. These will enable him to break even. In growth, a new need appears. The next entry must be planned so that a family of related products can be developed. Then, as growth eventually slows into maturity, the control of costs will become a paramount need.

The progressive evolution of these needs throughout a customer's business life cycle is shown in Figure 3.

Satisfying the Growth-Business Manager A customer with a start-up business will be satisfied only when the business achieves market entry on time and on budget. A customer with a new entry business will be satisfied only when the business achieves break-even on time and on budget so that positive cash flow can accrue. A customer with fast growth will be satisfied only when the business

FIGURE 3. LIFE-CYCLE NEEDS.

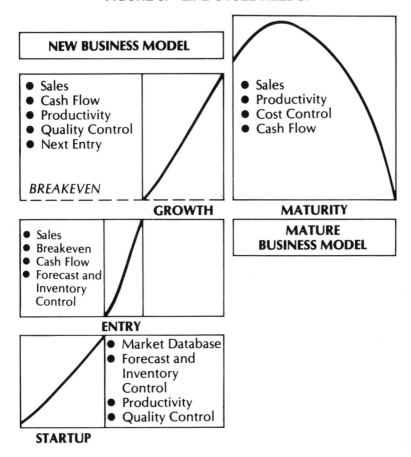

achieves and maintains a high rate of earnings apprecia-tion, a leadership position, and a dominant market share. Along the way, a customer with any of these three types of growth businesses will seek to satisfy several sub-objec-tives.

How proficient are you in satisfying a customer's growth managers? Your answer will largely depend on how good you are at helping them to sell. How fast can you help them get their products to market? With how much quality assurance? With what competitive advan-tage? How rapidly can you help them build share of market? How can you ensure against interruptions in production or, even worse, the specter of recall? Can you help them capitalize on their market acceptance by generating successive new extensions of their original products?

Satisfying the Mature-Business Manager   A customer with a mature business will be satisfied only if the business can maintain sufficient profitability to merit continued funding. This will require him to support his margins under fierce competitive pressure. He will have to manufacture and sell in sufficient volume to minimize his costs yet resist customer demands to continually discount his price.

In maturity, customers must maximize sales while minimizing costs. Because maximizing sales can increase costs—and because minimizing costs in vital support functions can decrease sales—managing a mature business is a paradox. Business continuity depends on resolving the paradox by determining the minimum cost base that will maximize sales.

How proficient are you in satisfying a customer's mature-business managers? Your answer will largely depend on how good you are at helping them reduce costs. How much expense can you squeeze out of their operations? How much can you help them avoid from the outset? How can you help them increase their productivity, lower their scrap rate, or subtract from their labor content, their inventory cost, or their need to finance their purchases from you on their balance sheets?

Depending on the business that you yourself are in, you may be able to satisfy customers who are in all four phases of their commercial life. Or you may be limited by your capabilities or your sense of mission to specialize in only one or some life-cycle phases. You will have to decide what you are best at doing. This will determine your core market.

At each phase of their business lives, your customers will want satisfaction. The start-up customer will be satisfied only if what you do for him helps to achieve market entry. Nothing else matters. The customer who has already entered his market will be satisfied initially by reaching the break-even point. Until then, nothing else matters. After entry, customer satisfaction depends entirely on maintaining a consistently high rate of growth. Nothing else matters. At maturity, customers will be satisfied only by deferring margin erosion, lowering operating costs, or increasing share of market. Nothing else matters.

What Type of Supplier Are You?

Strategy for a Single-Product Supplier

If you sell a single product to a single market, you are accepting the highest risk as a satisfier. If you fail, you fail completely. You have no compensating product or market to fall back on and usually no second chance with a market that you disappoint. Yet, because you have the advantage of concentration on your side, you also have the highest potential for being the best satisfier.

Concentration has been called the mother of success. With only one product and one market to concern you, an unparalleled opportunity exists for you to match your market's needs for satisfaction with your product's capabilities. This advantage is the advantage of the specialist, the supplier who specializes in maximizing the satisfaction of a specific market.

From a market's perspective, a specialist is a dedicated supplier who is wholly and irrevocably devoted to its satisfaction. The specialist's knowledge of customers' needs is exhaustive. He should possess the most accurate set of industry norms for his market. His ability to apply his strengths to meet the norms must be reliable; he must be able to achieve them the first time, every time. When the question is asked, "Is he so good because he is a specialist?" the answer must be, "He is the specialist because he is so good."

The specialist declares himself by means of his norms. They prove that he knows his customers and what it takes to satisfy them. With his norms, he can penetrate a customer's activities or operations and detect which of them depart from his norms. "That operation is too labor intensive," he can say. "It can benefit by reallocating one worker. This will save you $35,000 a year every year in fully loaded costs, beginning at once."

"This scrap rate is unnecessarily high by about a third," or, "This inventory system is acting as a drag on sales by a minimum of $100,000 a year," or, "This market is being undersold by at least one-quarter of its current contribution." The specialist can say these things with authority because he can compare what he sees with what he knows it should be. This ability is the secret of his value. Customers pay him premium prices for his knowledge of what should be and his ability to convert their operations to correlate more closely with it.

Due to the specialist's unique combination of expertise and market experience, he should be able to add the greatest amount of value in the shortest amount of time with the greatest amount of reliability. In other words, he should be the most satisfactory supplier and his market should contain its industry's most highly satisfied customers. They should be satisfied because of the amount of value they receive and the enhanced time value of its early onset. But they will be especially satisfied with its reliability, which they will come to depend on. When he promises to add to their value, they know that he will deliver.

The essence of the specialist is the reliable delivery of his normative values. Without norms, there would be no way to evaluate results. How could customers determine the goodness or badness of the specialist's contribution if no one knew what the optimum was? Similarly, without reliability, who would tamper with an ongoing situation if there were no way that its improvement could be assured in advance? Only reliability makes a promise of improvement worth the paper it is written on.

The symbiotic relationship between a single product or single market supplier and his market is based on reliability. The suppler must be the single most reliable source of added values. His customers will then be a reliable source of profits for him.

Strategy for a Multiproduct Supplier

If you sell multiple products to the same market you are inviting the highest rewards as a satisfier. If you succeed across the board you succeed grandly. Each product will be a success in its own right. In addition to their individual contribution to your TCS, their combined effect is cumulative. You have the advantages of positive cross-referencing on your side. If you are successful in relating your products to each other, a positive reference for one can act as a positive reference for another or for them all.

Just as positive cross-references among a family or products can be mutually beneficial, the downside effect of negative cross-referencing can be mutually devastating. One product's significant failure to satisfy can reflect adversely on the other members of its product family. All can suffer from the failings of one. This is especially true if the failure to satisfy is perceived as a pervasive corporate problem rather than as an isolated problem affecting only one of your products.

If you are a multiproduct supplier, you must therefore be adept at two skills. One is the creation of a family of products. This will give you synergy, the easily measured benefits of shared physical distribution and advertising, and more comprehensive sales opportunities. The other skill you will require is a talent for damage control, so that a problem with one product will not readily contaminate another. Each product will necessarily share your family surname. But each should have enough individual product persona to be accepted on its own merits as well as because of its family heritage.

Up to a certain number of products in a multiproduct line, the opportunistic advantages of synergy and economies of scale—as well as the increased revenues and earnings from scale—outweigh the increased risk that dissatisfaction with a single product will negatively affect TCS with the entire family of products. Beyond that certain number, the risks begin to outweigh the rewards. The "certain number" at which this takes place varies from company to company and industry to industry, but it can always be found at the same point. The critical factor that determines where predictable risk begins to exceed potential reward is the point where a multiproduct line starts to expand into the 80 percent of its products that yield only 20 percent or less of its profits.

Why is this point the danger point? It creates an ever-increasing likelihood of dissatisfaction because it begins to violate the principle of concentration. It is not simply that managers cannot focus the required attention on all the products in a multiproduct line because of their sheer volume alone. It is that a proliferation of products in the 80 percent category will decreasingly merit concentration based on their contribution.

Because they produce so small a percentage of total profits from sales, disproportionate attention to them cannot be justified. Abnormal care and concern, which are the minimum daily requirements for higher customer satisfaction, will be economically unjustifiable. So will allocation of the best managers. The historic rule of thumb has always made it clear that commodity products deserve only commodity care and commodity managers to administer it. There is no other way they can show even a small consistent profit.

All businesses sooner or later get into trouble as they multiply their commodity product lines. Companies that stay with simple line extensions incur the smallest risk. Apparently there can be innumerable extensions of Jell-O, for example, without seriously challenging their ability to be managed in a concentrated manner. But if you deal in more exotic products, such as sophisticated electronic hardward and software systems or personal financial services, as well as expansions from established product lines into new businesses, you should proceed cautiously. When a product becomes "another flavored desert" or "another computer system," a warning signal should flash that the perils of minimum satisfaction may be just around the corner.

Multiproduct businesses that seek high TCS ratings should limit the number of products in their commodity lines and focus on the creation, perpetuation, and extension of "brands." A brand is the opposite of a commodity. It offers unique value that is not replicated by competition, either in terms of the type of value it represents or the degree to which it is present. A brand's value is its ability to enhance a customer by adding its value to him and helping him achieve superiority, or at least overcome inferiority, in an area of importance to him. The enhanced customer becomes more satisfied with himself and therefore with the brand that enhances him.

Because brands offer high user values, they can command high prices. This makes them earnings leaders, contributors to the 80 percent of all earnings that come from only 20 percent or so of all the products in a line. For this reason, they should make prior claim on the concentration of your corporate time, talent, and resources. This gives them the best chance to be high satisfiers.

Maximizing Satisfaction for Single and Multiple Lines

If you are a single-product supplier who has established yourself as the satisfaction leader in your market, you are undercapitalizing the satisfaction you have created. To capitalize it more fully, you can diversity into related branded products that can also be covered by your specialist's umbrella positioning. As long as you stay with brands and retain your specialist rating for adding satisfactory value to your customers, you will be reducing your single-product risk and increasing your reward. Because you have been suffering opportunity loss from your under-utilized capacity to produce satisfaction, your diversification should be exceedingly cost effective.

Your safest diversifications will be complementary and supplementary products that allow you to add more value to the same or closely related customer activities or operations in which you already specialize. These will let you soak up the surplus satisfaction available to you in the market. At brand prices, they should have a high incremental value to you.

As a multiproduct supplier, you have a different mission to maximize satisfaction. You must play the role of the specialist in each of the product families that you brand. This will give you some of the same advantages of single-product suppliers and will better enable you to compete against them. Like them, you will have to choose each of your multiple niches carefully and make sure that you can really bring a specialist's expertise and experience to all of your markets. They will judge you the same way they evaluate anyone who approaches them from a specialist position. Can these people satisfy my need for incremental value? Can they maximize my satisfaction? Do they have norms for improving my situation? Do they have the capabilities to bring me closer to the norms? Can they do it at a high, quick, and reliable rate of return on my investment?

As single-product suppliers diversify into brand families and as multiproduct suppliers become increasingly specialized, they resemble each other more closely to their core customers. Each offers himself as a specialist in the same customer activities and operations. Each is able to bring to bear on a customer's situation a family of solutions. The advantages and disadvantages of smallness and bigness will be at least partially neutralized. Who will win? In other words, who will be able to supply the highest satisfaction? The winner will always be the sup- plier who most reliably can bring his customers the clos- est to their industry norms or, even better, help to exceed them. This ability is independent of supplier size. It de- pends on two things: possessing authentic customer knowledge and applying professional implementation skills to put that knowledge to work. If you choose to be a multiproduct supplier through strategic alliances with other manufacturers, these criteria should be among your paramount considerations.

Your Manufacturing Strategy

Quality is a perception. Like all business perceptions, it exists in the eyes of your users. Although it is perceptual, it is founded on realities. A product cannot be perceived to work well unless workability has been engineered into its design and manufacture. It cannot have durability unless it has been made to last; reliability unless it has been made free from defects; nor can it have flexibility unless it has been made with multiple uses in mind.

The single most important perception about a product is its value. This is the worth that it can add to the existing worth of its users. Everything must be done to establish this value, and nothing must be allowed to compromise it. It is imperative that no negative value be permitted to intrude on the positive values of any one of your products. Nothing will dissatisfy a customer more than a major problem that cannot be resolved or cannot be resolved cost-effectively. In other words, it becomes more trouble than it is worth. For this reason, you must follow a policy of *no negatives.*

No negatives is the flip side of the responsibility of manufacturing strategy whose main side is to build in the single most important value as determined by your mar- ket. A product that bears the single most important posi- tive value and is free from important contrary values that can negate it is a good bet to provide a high level of satisfaction. Subsidiary values are important if they are additive. But they are no substitute for the single most important value if it is lacking.

The ultimate downside of manufacturing strategy is product recall. This is a three-way disaster. First, recall deprives your market of a product's value, forcing substitutes on it and, at the same time, instilling doubts about the product's capability to satisfy. Second, recall deprives your distribution of the product's value by taking it off the market and leaving a void in its place. Third, your own profit from the product is lost, replaced instead by added costs that serve to subtract from your past earnings and prejudice future ones. Instead of an added profit of, say, $100,000, a cost of $100,000 is incurred. Your total loss only begins at $200,000, growing sizably by the loss of the invested value of the $100,000 profits and the opportunity loss of the $100,000 costs that you could have allocated more productively elsewhere.

Zero defects is the manufacturing strategy best calculated to ensure against recall. The quality assurance on which a zero-defects policy is based is an essential ingredient in creating satisfaction in the marketplace. But quality is not simply a criterion of your product's performance. It must be considered as your customer's standard, reflecting the quality of the value received from performance rather than the operating attributes of performance itself.

The stereotyped caveat that quality must be "built in and not added on" is the formula for manufacturing's contribution to satisfaction. This is the best guarantee that the specifications of customer satisfaction will be met in the manufacturing process: *how much* value will prove to be extractable from the product, *how soon* it can become available, and *how sure* the customer can be that the value will accrue in exactly that amount and within that exact time frame.

The imposition of customer standards of satisfaction on the manufacturing process is the keystone to quality as your customers perceive it and accept it. In this sense, quality assurance means satisfaction assurance. It does not mean simply that the product works better as a result. A dedicated facility is not one that is just devoted to a single product. It is singularly dedicated to the specifications of customer satisfaction so that whatever goes out the door does not come back.

Finally, "made to last" is not only a claim for durability. It is a pledge to lasting satisfaction because customer values have become inherent in your manufacturing operation. Some companies like to say of their manufacturing operations that "Customerese is spoken here." Others take it a step further with the objective that "Better customers—not just better products—are made here".

Your Advertising Strategy

Advertising, and the sales promotion that is allied to it, is the supreme agent of customer satisfaction. It has the ability to outperform even your product or service itself. The unique capability that sets advertising apart is that it, and it alone, can create a customer's anticipation of satisfaction before purchase and use. In this way, advertising more than predisposes your sales. It predisposes satisfaction in advance of sales.

The objectives of your advertising should be twofold: First, it must create satisfaction before use. Second, it must encourage reuse. Advertising allows nonusers to experience the satisfaction of use vicariously, at no risk. It then reassures users that their satisfaction is a standard experience, shared by other users, and therefore repeatable. In both cases, advertising makes satisfaction predictable.

How does advertising do this? By saying, "Here are the benefits that will add value to you. If you are a consumer, here is how your health will improve, how your beauty will be enhanced, how your personal wealth will be increased or safeguarded, how your convenience will be multiplied. If you are a business customer, here is how your costs will be reduced or how your revenues will be raised." Telling *how* is central to advertising success. But the *how* must not focus on how your product is made or how it works. It must concentrate on *how the user is made more satisfied.*

Advertising is the blueprint for customer satisfaction. It alerts its market to future values that will be added to its activities or operations. At its best, it replicates an exchange of confidences between a trusted source and a trusting prospect. Who can be trusted? The most trustworthy source is never you, the manufacturer or supplier. *The most credible persuader is another customer who has already been satisfied.* This permits new customers to identify with the same satisfaction, apply it to their own situation, and rehearse their enjoyment of its benefits for themselves.

The wisest advice that you can give to a prospective customer is to talk to a satisfied user. Your advertising must approximate this approach as closely as possible. It must act as word-of-mouth in print or video. One of your satisfied users must talk to another. "Here is my new value," he or she must say. "Compare it to my previous value. The difference measures my satisfaction."

There is no substitute for testimonial advertising in creating or reinforcing satisfaction. Testimonials are miniature case histories. They evidence reality. They answer the questions "Does the product work?" "Will I like it?" "Is it for me?" with demonstrable results from users for whom it is working and who like it—users in situations so similar to their own that nonusers can know it will work satisfactorily for them as well.

Every satisfied user is a prospective testifier. Every prospective user is his or her constituent. Once satisfied, he or she becomes the next prospective testifier. The more testimonials that you can accumulate, the easier it will be to develop *standards of satisfaction* from your products, services, and systems. It will be to your immense advantage to advertise these standards as your proprietary values and to advertise yourself as the standard-bearer for your customers' activities and operations. Your advertising can then adopt the "if-then" strategy. *If* you want to add these standard values, *then* we are the best source of help.

If you are dedicated to scoring consistently high on TCS among your important customers, you must become the advertised industry standard of satisfaction. The levels of satisfaction that you can produce must be the norms that your customers aspire to achieve and work with you to maintain. Advertising should be the conveyor of your standards. There is nothing more important for you to advertise. Nothing says more about you as a satisfier. If you do not possess the industry standards, neither will your customers. The only thing you will be able to advertise at that point will be your products. You will be wasting advertising to talk about yourself. Who other than you will be interested?

When you advertise through the testimony of satisfied customers who document their satisfaction with what you have done for them, what kind of audience can you expect for your advertising? You can expect that the most devoted audience will be the customers you have already satisfied. They will consume your advertising because it will be, in effect, *their* advertising. They will consume it in order to reinforce their satisfaction. It will be the familiar case of the saved coming forward to hear more about salvation. How many times and in how many ways, you may ask, do satisfied customers want to be satisfied by us again? The answer is forever. If being satisfied once is good, twice is better. If being satisfied in one activity or business function is good, two are better. The satisfied are insatiable for satisfaction. They know its benefits. And they know where to get them.

The second most dedicated audience for your advertising will most likely be prospective customers who identify with customers you are already satisfying, who can project your benefits onto their own situations, and who want to or need to obtain them quickly. The third audience will be customers who have previously been satisfied by one of your competitors but who have been made dissatisfied by the comparison of their current standards with yours.

The first group (current satisfied customers) you must seek to reinforce and recycle. The second group (prospective customers) you must seek to enroll. The third group (your competitors' customers) you must seek to convert.

It is obvious that satisfaction must precede purchase and repurchase. Customers buy from an expectation of being satisfied, not to find out if they will be. In the same way that a customer must already be satisfied before he will buy again, a prospect must expect to be satisfied before he will buy at all. With a customer it is easy to understand how repurchase is satisfaction-dependent. But how can someone who has never bought from you be sufficiently expectant of being satisfied to want to become your customer?

The creation of expected satisfaction before use—the belief that partnering with you is the best if not the only thing to do—entails three steps:

1. *Creating testimonial advertising based on case histories of users you have satisfied in the customer's own industry.* This gives prospects a standard of comparison with their own activities or operations.
2. *Providing a specific proposal of comparative benefits and costs for the improvement of the customer's own situation.* This gives prospects a customized comparison, specifying the difference between their current level of satisfaction and the enhanced level that can result from working with you.
3. *Making a sale based on the value of the difference.*

A prospect who becomes your customer because he expects to be satisfied with you is well on the way to becoming a satisfied customer. In effect, his first use will be a reuse because he has rehearsed his satisfaction with you in advance.

Your Sales Force Allocation Strategy

Sophisticated sales strategy maximizes the allocation of manpower and support resources. But where is that? Is it with new prospects or with already-satisfied customers? Is it with predisposed prospects or with cold ones? Is it with highly satisfied customers or with the "low satisfieds?"

Your prime sales force—the men and women who have the maximum capability to satisfy—should always be allocated to customers who are already among your "high satisfieds." The objective of the sales force will be to satisfy those customers even more a second time, and then a third, and on and on. How can a satisfied customer be satisfied even more? There are two ways. The customer can be satisfied to a greater degree in the same activity or operation. Or the customer can be satisfied in another activity or operation. In the first instance, you can enhance the original satisfaction. In the second instance, you can migrate from it.

No customer is primed for additional satisfaction more than a customer who is already satisfied. He has the strongest motivation of all to do business with you: He has proof that you can satisfy him. He is his own testifier in your behalf. There is nothing that you can sell him that he cannot sell himself on even better. You have the optimal reference, the maximum credibility, and the readiest partner.

A satisfied customer is your most precious resource. Once you have achieved his satisfaction you should ask yourself, "How can we improve it?" Once you have improved it, you should ask, "Where else can we satisfy him?" The answers to these questions will determine your joint partnership plan. They will also help forecast your own growth plan, suggesting the products and services you will require in order to protect your satisfaction leadership from opportunity loss—the cost in lost revenues and profits of underserving a satisfied customer who is a prime prospect for added satisfaction.

To permit a market segment of highly satisfied customers to remain undercapitalized in the satisfaction that you could be delivering to them is the most unforgiveable sin of sales management. Yet that is precisely what sales managers allow to happen time and again by emphasizing volume sales spread "horizontally" across many customers instead of volume sales concentrated with the customers they can best satisfy. "Sell something to everybody" is a strategy for dissatisfaction, not satisfaction. It leads to satisfying a few customers a little and dissatisfying—or, at the least, failing to fully satisfy—the rest. This is the curse of vendor sales strategies where an order is an order regardless of where it comes from, where a unit sold is a unit sold and a dollar earned is a dollar earned, and where customers are just as interchangeable as their vendors.

There is a vital difference between selling to build customer satisfaction and selling to build market share. In the first instance, you sell to a customer so that you can sell to him again and again. In the second instance, you sell only to go on to sell to some one else. This difference is symbolized in the sales manager's response to the sales representative who has just made a major sale that has satisfied a customer. "Now get out and go sell someone else the same thing." A very different reply is this one: "Move in and take up residence there to ensure satisfaction, to upgrade it and migrate it." This is the policy of customer satisfaction.

As a group, your most satisfied customers (the "high satisfieds") will never amount to more than 20 percent or less of all your customers. But the power of your ability to satisfy them is so great that they will account for up to 80 percent of your profits. They, and the "high predisposeds," who are your best prospects for future high satisfaction, compose the core of your market. They deserve, and require, the concentration of your best sales resources.

Every time you undersatisfy a "high satisfied" customer, you are leaving money on the table. You may also be leaving a major customer vulnerable to competition. Every time you fail to convert or underconvert a "high predisposed" customer, you are walking away from a future major customer. Nothing must be allowed to take precedence over capitalizing your "satisfieds" and converting your "predisposeds." No customers are as cost effective for you to sell to or as profitable for you to partner with. If you satisfy them to the fullest extent, no other customers can rival their importance. If you neglect your mission of satisfying them to the fullest, no other customers can make up for your loss. All others will be costlier for you to sell to, and you will be less effective in satisfying them.

If you drive yourself by the objective of customer satisfaction, you will always know where your sales force is. You will always know, too, how to take the mystery out of segmenting your major customer markets. Who must your major accounts be?

1. Your primary customers must always be the customers you are already satisfying. Your mission with them must be to satisfy them even more.
2. Your secondary customers must always be the prospects who are already predisposed to be satisfied by you. Your mission with them must be the same: to satisfy them even more.

There is a simple overriding reason why these two types of customers compose your core market. *You are able to satisfy them best.* Their needs and your capabilities come together in such a way that you can add greater value to them than anyone else can and they can add greater value to you in return. This is the kind of natural partnership that predicts satisfaction. No search is more urgent for you than to identify your natural satisfaction partners. This should be the first order of every business that is starting up or entering a growth period or becoming recompetitive by restructuring. It answers the question, "When we get in the car to make our first sales call each day, where should we go?" It also answers the next question: "When we get there what should we say?"

What of the 80 percent of all customers who, by exclusion, you have calculated will yield only 20 percent or so of your profits? It must not be your policy to maximize their satisfaction. If they are maximally satisfied by the business they do with you, it will be coincidental. But your policy will only be to serve them, not satisfy them to their maximal level.

Naturally, you will not do anything to dissatisfy them. You will simply not staff your sales force, support it, or allocate its time and talent to deliver the same quality of satisfaction that you commit to your core market of "satisfieds" and "predisposeds." Even if you tried to maximally satisfy the other 80 percent of your market, you would not be likely to succeed. Even if you succeed, you would not be likely to profit from them in any way commensurate with the profits from your core market. And while you were trying, you would be putting your "satisfieds" and "predisposeds" at risk of reduced satisfaction and thereby imperiling the very foundation of your business.

Coping With a Maintenance Mode

When you find that your satisfaction score is rising, either in a single element or across the board in totality, you can be fairly certain that what is happening is cause and effect. You are delivering added satisfaction and the customer is validating it. You are building momentum. The most obvious strategy is to increase it, to see how high "up" is and to take advantage of Newton's Law that motion tends to persevere. This is exactly what you must do.

When you find "up," or think you have found it, what then?

It will be tempting for you to say, "Things are going good; why change?" As soon as you do, you will be exposed. You will be making yourself vulnerable to competition.

From a competitor's point of view, there are two prime situations for making missionary sales. One is at the lowest point in a customer's satisfaction with a rival supplier. The other is at the prolongation of the highest point, where no change has occurred for some time. The customer is obviously satisfied. But over time he begins to suspect that he may be missing something—something technically innovative or a new market-penetration strategy. In such an unstable situation, a customer is open to seduction by the latest management fad, perhaps even something as ephemeral as a search for excellence. If you have been doing well with the customer but have not been able to do better, and then the customer leaves you for a competitor, you will be inclined to mark it off to the "What have you done for me lately?" syndrome. What the customer will really be asking, however, is something like, "Is there satisfaction beyond where we are now?"

No matter how highly satisfied your customer is, once he plateaus for any length of time you are in danger. You should constantly seek improvement in satisfying a core customer's "must" factors; never leave well enough alone, because your competitors will not. If an incremental improvement is difficult, you should dare to experiment with innovative strategies even at the risk of temporarily lowering satisfaction. This allows the customer to qualify his suspicion of opportunity loss, proving to himself that there is none, and looking to you for innovation instead of to your competitors. The best response that any customer of yours can make to a competitor who tries to take him away from you is, "Yes, we know, we have already tried that."

The concept of a maintenance mode, then, becomes one of maintaining the aggressively innovative satisfaction strategies that helped you to achieve maximum TCS in the first place. There is no rest at the top; there is only vulnerability. *If you remember how you got there, you have the best chance to stay there.* You will also know how a competitor can get there.

Looking for New Opportunities

What should you look for to sense the opportunity to compete for a customer's satisfaction? And what should you do when you think you have found it? A three-part method will bring the best results.

First, you should study your competitor's TCS scores from your market research. You should look for "must factors" where your competitors are scoring below the level of your norms. This tells you automatically that you may be able to do better and that prospective customers should be interested.

Second, you should look for "must factors" where a competitor's score is high but has been stagnant for several consecutive quarters. This tells you there may be the chance for you to do better and that prospective customers should be interested.

Third, you should propose to add improved values to a customer based on capturing the opportunity loss, or as much of it as possible, that he is now suffering. You should quantify this renewed opportunity, raising the customer's expectations closer to his suspicions. By representing opportunity, you may be able to reposition his current supplier from being the preferred satisfier to an unaffordable cost in terms of lost opportunities. "Yes, you are satisfied today. But there are new standards taking shape for tomorrow, some of which are already realizable today. We set the norms for those standards. We can help you make them your standards, too."

If you are going to represent yourself as the means to enhance the satisfaction of customers who are already adequately satisfied by your competitors, make the customer's cost in lost opportunities your major selling point. It is not enough merely to narrate a claim of his loss of opportunity. You must quantify it. Otherwise, opportunity remains a vague, vacuous concept whose existence may be alleged but, unless a dollar value can be attached to it, cannot be proven.

Customers ignore opportunity costs that they cannot quantify. Can you attach value to it? Customers cannot justify enduring opportunity cost once it has been quantified. Can you capture it for them?

What does it mean when a customer says that he is already satisfied? Perhaps he is already meeting or exceeding his industry norms and feels pretty good about his operations. Or perhaps he is satisfied by the relationship with his current supplier. As a third possibility, he may have become disenchanted with outside suppliers and is now satisfied to serve his needs with his own in-house operations. In such a case, he himself will be your competitor. If he is already in a "steady state" of satisfaction, should you leave him alone or try to satisfy him even more?

You will find the answer in your own norms. What does your experience tell you about the impact you can have on a business like the customer's—a business of comparable size, with comparable market position, similar operations, and in the same industry or one very much like it? Are your norms better than his current performance? If so, you can try to satisfy him even more. In this regard, your norms are the best yardstick you can have for determining if, and by how much, you can satisfy a customer. You can use them like a template, superimposing them on a customer's current performance to determine where your norms can offer greater satisfaction. If you can identify such areas, then you can start a sales cycle by presenting them.

In computers, as an example, competitors often find they run up against a stone wall when they call on a customer who identifies his company as an "IBM house." Such a customer is "perfectly happy" with IBM. Should competitors try to discover latent dissatisfactions or even try to create them? Or is it more successful for each of them to establish a private niche of expertise wherein the customer can become satisfied without challenge to IBM? This will require niche marketing, finding vertical opportunities that are subsumed in IBM's horizontal dominance and staking a claim to one or more of them.

This process must be managed in exactly the same way that IBM's consolidation has taken place: by selling from norms of superior satisfaction.

The norms presentation process is a 1-2-3 sequence. First, you reveal your norms. They become a focal point of your approach to a customer, speaking for your expertise as owners of the customer's industry standards. Norms give you credibility. They testify that you know the customer's business. Even more, they certify that you know how to apply your business to the customer's business so that new values can be added to it.

The second step is to invite the customer to compare his current performance against your norms. Where is he deficient? By how much? What would it be worth to him if his performance could be brought into closer conformity with your norms? If the value he foresees is significant, you can take your process to the third step by proposing how you can help the customer more closely approach the norms. How much closer can he come? How long will it take? What investment will be required and what kind of rate will it return?

The theme of your norms presentation should never be self-serving. You must not say, "*We* can do better for you." The only theme that is consonant with customer satisfaction is to say to the customer, "*You* can be better. *You* can add more value to your business." As a result, the customer's performance will be more satisfactory, it will cost him less, or it will be more productive in units of efficiency or revenues.

Mismanagement's Reward: Getting Fired

When your satisfaction rating declines, the two easiest things for you to do are almost always wrong. One is to blame the customer: He is unappreciative, he has no loyalty, all he ever wanted to do was use us anyway, the new people in charge have none of the character or ethics of the former management. The second thing is to put the blame on your competitors: They don't play by the rules, they buy business instead of selling it, they know someone we don't know, they regularly cut corners on quality and service in order to shave their price. All of these allegations may be true. But when satisfaction declines, it is generally your own fault.

A core customer is yours to hold or lose. You start from the favored position. You are, after all, already in place. You know his people and their needs. They know your people and their capabilities. You are already satisfying them to some extent. The customer has a stake in being further satisfied by you just as you have a stake in further satisfying him. Each of you has made a considerable investment in the other. You are reluctant to write it off. Yet a customer will write it off if he can calculate that the cost of sustaining lower levels of satisfaction than he believes necessary has become excessive.

He will give up what he has, however significant, for what he must have because it is more significant.

What have you been doing wrong? There are two possible answers to this question. The most likely answer is that you have misperceived his "must list," his priorities for the prime objectives he must currently achieve. You have been concentrating on the wrong things, satisfying him in general but overlooking what he counts the most. You are costing him the opportunity to achieve them. In this way you become a luxury and therefore unaffordable.

The second answer is that you have accurately perceived his "must list" but you are too slow in delivering the satisfactions you have proposed. Perhaps you are ponderous or indecisive. Perhaps you bungle. The customer's loss comes from the time value of money as each day sees him still far from realizing his objectives. Waiting will eventually become unaffordable and he will act to cut his loss by cutting his relationship with you.

Whether you are doing the wrong things or doing the right things cost-ineffectively, the customer who is losing opportunities for enhancing his value will do you in. He cannot help it. He has no choice but to maximize his opportunities. They are always few and fleeting; their windows close all too quickly and there is no assurance that they will either open again or be superseded by other opportunities that are equally attractive and affordable.

So, in spite of what you have done in the past and what you may be doing right now in the present, customers will leave you because of what you are not doing. That is why it is easy to accuse them of "never being satisfied, no matter what we do for them" or "always wanting more." There is no way that customers can be satisfied if you are not doing what counts most to them. They will always want more if what you are giving them is not what they want most.

You will be undone not by what you do but by what you do not do. You can score high on satisfaction for what you do, but at the same time, you can incur low satisfaction or even dissatisfaction for what you do not do. This should not make you cynical about customer loyalty. All customers are loyal. But they are loyal to their own objectives, not to yours.

They are grateful to suppliers who have been helpful in the past, and may even be nostalgic for them, but they will not be loyal to what has gone before if it is not going on now.

It is your responsibility to discern your customers' priority objectives and to become every bit as loyal to them as your customers are. That is what partners have for each other—loyalty to the same objectives and the same time frame for realizing them. Past associations carry over only so far. Suppliers tend to expect them to go on forever. When they are taken by surprise one day by being fired, they are stunned. They can think only of the good job they have been doing. "Why, only the other day," the president of Buick's advertising agency said when he was summarily dismissed, "they were telling me what a great guy I was." What they did not tell him, of course, was what a great opportunity loss they thought he was costing them.

The principal risk you run as a satisfier is that you will succeed where it does not count and fail where it counts. This is why you must be expert in knowing "where it counts" and in how to be successful there. These are the basic tools of your survival kit. Of the two, it may be surprising that knowing where it counts is even more important to the longevity of your customers' satisfaction than being an unfailing expert in adding value to it. Customers will sometimes tolerate your adding a little less value than they have bargained for. They may also tolerate your being a little late in helping them achieve full payback on their investment with you. They will be tolerant about these failings as long as they know that you are working hard, that you have not made any egregious errors of commission or omission, and they can see signs that you are helping them move on to their major objectives.

A supplier that satisfies the 80 percent of things that do not count as "musts" and fails to satisfy the 20 percent of the things that make or break a relationship is in the wrong business. Somewhere among the nonessentials he is good at satisfying are the essential "must factors" for other customers in other businesses. Who, he should ask, are these customers? Where are they? If he can find them, he is already well on his way to satisfying them.

Very few suppliers get fired for doing the right things less than perfectly. But practically all suppliers who are fired will find that they are being rewarded for doing the wrong things well or taking too long to do the right ones. "If we had just known what you really wanted" is no excuse. Nor is "if we only had a little more time." A supplier's premium price is earned by knowing the hot buttons in his customers' businesses and compressing the time it takes to improve them.

You must learn that you can satisfy a customer in many ways but still be unsatisfactory to him. You must also learn that you can *not* satisfy a customer in many ways but still be satisfactory. Throwing a handful of solutions at a customer's problems will rarely lead to satisfaction. Conversely, taking careful aim at one or two objectives and hitting each selected target on time the first time leads directly to satisfaction and to the invitation to do it again.

There is an old saying to this effect: There are many satisfied current customers; there are many dissatisfied former customers; but there are no dissatisfied current customers for very long.

This captures for you the essence of what you need to know. *Customers do not leave you as much as you leave them when you leave them dissatisfied.*

3

Measuring Customer Satisfaction

Customer satisfaction must be managed to achieve a single objective: to improve your customers' value. Your measurements of customer satisfaction must respond to this mission, concerning itself with the types and degrees of improvement you make in the value of customer operations and activities.

The measurement of customer satisfaction is therefore based on auditing *improvement*. Essentially, you must measure three things: (1) what you improve, (2) how much you improve it, and (3) how much better you improve it than your competitors. This approach to satisfaction gives it an activist interpretation. It says that you satisfy your customers by enabling your customers to do things better for themselves.

In this way, you can come up with a useful definition of

a competitor: someone who can improve the same customer operation or activity that you improve, and can do it as well as or better than you. He may have the same products or services or he may not. His benefits may be based on the same or different capabilities. From the customer's point of view, the means are irrelevant. Only the result matters. In a similar manner, you can define a customer as someone whose operations or activities you can improve as well as or better than a competitor can. Your key customers, the only customers whose satisfaction must be your preoccupation, are those whose operations or activities you can improve best: those to whom you can give the greatest value for the greatest return.

Delivering Added Value

Improving the value of a customer's operation to his business or the value of an activity to his lifestyle is a matter of implementation. The only value you represent to a customer is implemented value. Your reputation as a value-adder with other customers is valueless unless you can implement new value for each new customer. Your products delivered to a customer's receiving dock on time and without defects are valueless unless you can implement them by installing them and training the customer's people to use them in the optimal manner. Your services are valueless unless you can implement them to decrease a customer's downtime or scrap rate or inventory stockout or falloff in market share.

The most dissatisfying experiences for customers are with suppliers who promise to deliver breakthrough products and then fail to produce the goods or cannot get them to market on time. It is not that customers are unforgiving. Nor are they unaware of the vagaries of R&D. It is simply that they count on the benefits that a supplier promises, building them into their plans and projections as, many times, the basis for their own breakthroughs. Suddenly, they are defeated. The supplier, although defeated himself, nonetheless must bear the brunt of their frustrations.

The best rule for customer satisfaction is *to deliver*. There is a vital corollary to this proposition. It is *not to promise what cannot be delivered*. Disappointment can be a lower low than fulfillment can be a high.

It is commonplace to forget an expectation that has been fulfilled. Hardly any customer forgets a disappointment. In the long run, what is expected but not received counts stronger negatively than fulfillment counts positively.

Customer satisfaction is the prime deliverable. "How reliably we deliver it best" must be the focal point of your measurement process. The focus in measurement must therefore be on active verbs: the action elements that express your initiative in delivering, installing, implementing, servicing, improving productivity and profits, improving profitable sales volume and market share— whatever it is that you are positioned to do best. The most active verb when you speak in the vocabulary of customer satisfaction is *to improve*. You must be the best improvers in the areas of your capabilities. No one must be better.

The "What" and the "When" of Measuring

There are two factors that determine what you need to measure and how often you need to measure it. One is the life-cycle phase of your business. The newer you are, the more frequently you will need to evaluate how well you are satisfying your customers. Early large-scale dissatisfaction, or even a "ho-hum" level of satisfaction, can be fatal. On the other hand, if you are a well-established business you can often ride out temporary aberrations in your track record.

The second factor determining what and when you must measure is the type of business you are in. If your customers make daily decisions about your products or services and yesterday's dissatisfaction can have an immediate impact on today's sales, you will have to measure more frequently than a business whose sales cycle takes longer. For this reason, Federal Express measures customer satisfaction monthly, IBM tests its markets quarterly, and AT&T uses yearly evaluations supplemented by special studies at times of change in its customer relations.

IBM and AT&T are two companies that follow a zero-base strategy for measuring satisfaction. They go into their markets as few times as necessary. By way of contrast, Federal Express is in the kind of business that must know what is going on day by day. Companies like Federal Express need plenty of warning to take remedial action if they find that satisfaction is slipping away or their principal competitor, United Parcel Service, is gaining on them. In this regard, Federal Express is typical of many consumer products and service companies whose business is always up for grabs whenever a competitive innovation is introduced, prices change, or a customer has an unhappy experience.

Measurement Scales

In order to quantify satisfaction so that it can be measured on an objective basis, companies use a variety of different scales. They vary in the terms they employ and in the number of points they establish, some measuring in the equivalent of yards or feet while others measure inches, and some subdividing inches into microns.

101-Point Scales

Companies in a consumer-type business like Federal Express need to monitor microshifts in customer sentiment to see if they will go on to become leading indicators of trends. Federal Express uses an intricate measurement scale of 101 points, ranging from 100, which represents *complete satisfaction*, to zero, which represents *complete dissatisfaction*.

5-Point Scales

IBM, whose business is very different, finds it sufficient to rely on a 5-point scale that ranges from *very satisfied* and *satisfied* on one end through *neutral* in the middle to *dissatisfied* and *very dissatisfied* on the other end. By adding together the number of very satisfied and satisfied customers, IBM calculates its percentage of satisfied customers.

Like IBM, Cablevision also uses a 5-point measurement scale that compares the percentage of customers who are strongly satisfied, rating Cablevision *excellent* or *good*, with the percentage who rate Cablevision as *not too satisfactory* or *poor*. In the middle of the scale is *satisfactory*.

10-Point Scales

General Electric's (GE) 10-point scale falls between the 101-point measurement of Federal Express and the 5-point scales of IBM and Cablevision. GE measures satisfaction on a category-by-category basis along a scale that runs from *poor* (valued at 1) through *excellent* (10). For every category, GE also measures its importance from *not important at all* (1) through *extremely important* (10).

The types of scales used by Federal Express, IBM, Cablevision and GE are shown in Figure 4.

4-Point & 5-Point Scales

Figure 4 also shows a scale that can measure satisfaction at either 4 or 5 points. It is useful for multibrand companies whose products are constantly being com-

FIGURE 4.   TYPES OF SCALES FOR RATING CUSTOMER SATISFACTION.

101-POINT SCALE

0%   100%
Complete ————————————————————————— Complete
Dissatisfaction   Satisfaction

5-POINT SCALES

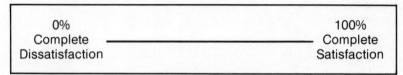

Excellent   Good   Satisfactory   Not Too   Poor
                                        Satisfactory

(Percentage Strongly Satisfied)   (Percentage Not Satisfied)

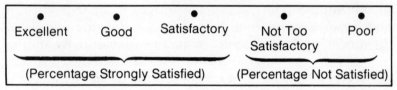

Very   Satisfied   Neutral   Dissatisfied   Very
Satisfied   Dissatisfied

(Percentage Satisfied)

4-POINT/5-POINT SCALE

Much   Better   About   Both Not
Better   the Same   Satisfactory

Much   Better   About   Not   Much
Better   the Same   as Good   Worse

10-POINT SCALE

Not Important   Extremely
   at All   Important
      1   2   3   4   5   6   7   8   9   10

      1   2   3   4   5   6   7   8   9   10
   Poor   Excellent

pared against each other or against the products of other suppliers. General Foods' several dry cereals and the many detergent products of Procter & Gamble can be compared against their internal and external competitors on a scale that allows them to be ranked from *much better* and *better* through *about the same* to *not so good* and *much worse*. A 4-point scale that attempts to serve the same purpose runs from *much better* to *better, about the same,* and *both not satisfactory.*

All these types of scales can be supplemented by the judicious use of open-ended questions that are designed to uncover the reasons underlying responses, whether they are negative or positive. Questioning can also try to determine if customers are aware of any trends leading to improving or worsening satisfaction or any emerging competitive satisfactions.

Measuring Attitudes and Activities

Measurements of customer attitudes are often disparaged as yielding only "soft numbers." Activity measurements based on buying behavior—how many units actually moved off the shelves—are, in contrast, regarded as "hard numbers" that leave no questions unanswered or any doubts to be resolved. What does it mean, managers frequently ask, to say that a customer is satisfied? Does that mean we can count on him to be a loyal repeat customer? No one knows. But to say that a customer *has bought* seems to say it all.

Yet buying and being satisfied can be two different things. In some industries, this is made clear. Customer complaints to automobile manufacturers provide tangible evidence of satisfaction's opposite, dissatisfaction. Since the mid-1980s, American manufacturers have been paying increasing attention to complaints. Plants in the United States have been revolutionized to keep problems down. A combination of automation and motivation has symbolized Detroit's new attitude, taking drastic action inside the factory as well as in the minds of the men and women who work there. The results show a 25 to 40 percent improvement in quality as measured by the number of defects per each 100 cars that are discovered while they are still on the assembly line. Expensive and sophisticated computerized control systems are being used to catch faulty parts before the car owner does. Relationships between manufacturers and their suppliers are also being revolutionized by the renaissance in customer satisfaction. At Ford, suppliers who make defect-free parts for twelve months running are signed to long-term exclusive contracts.

Consumer products manufacturers and service suppliers, with their dependence on relatively short, reflexive sale cycles and market sensitivity to advertising and price manipulations, are especially comfortable with activity measurements of customer satisfaction. Coffee makers can count the cans, cereal makers can tally the cartons, and telephone companies can calculate the usage rate of calls made every hour of every day, week in and week out. If satisfaction falls, sales will tell them about it when they also fall shortly after. When sales go up, they assume that satisfaction is also on the rise.

Makers of business products and suppliers of professional services, whether they are frequently acquired or need lengthy, well-considered sales cycles, are more likely to be concerned with interrelationships between sales and satisfaction. They have learned about the "sleeper effect" of dissatisfaction on their sales. They have also discovered the wisdom of identifying as early as possible even the slimmest slippages in their hold on customers. Once aware, they can correct declining satisfaction before it makes serious, perhaps irreversible, inroads.

It is precisely because business-to-business companies generally lack the daily volume of sales that are normal for consumer companies that they turn so readily to satisfaction measurements for help. Each major customer is vital. To lose a key piece of business can be irremediable in the short run. Not only are today's sales lost; tomorrow's follow-up sales are also forsaken. It may take three to five years to become competitive again with a dissatisfied customer who has sought satisfaction elsewhere. Meanwhile, someone else's key customer will have to be captured.

Nevertheless, for both consumer and business-to-business companies, there are compelling reasons why attitude measurement can be vital. Attitudes become negative before sales actually decline, so attitudes can serve an important early warning function. Attitude analysis also helps identify the key growth factors in a market that can act as the foundation for new sales. Attitudes are especially important in segmenting markets. While need differentiation is the traditional criterion for identifying a market, attitude differences can play a crucial role in defining the boundaries between segments of the heavy, repeat users who deserve your concentrated attention and the lighter, more sporadic customers who do not.

Attitude analysis is a critical tool for understanding your competitive positioning. How strong does your market perceive your competitors to be in the areas of your own strength? What are their comparative weaknesses? Do these weak points offer you an opportunity? If so, how much and how soon?

When you measure customer attitudes, you have the option to test the satisfaction levels of two types of customers. One, of course, is your own. The other is your competitors' customers, prospects who buy primarily or exclusively from rival suppliers. Is their satisfaction weakening? Does the opportunity exist for you to make an inroad or is the time not yet ripe? What is the basis for the longevity of the competitive relationship and how is it holding up under market changes, people changes, the effects of time, and your own competitive campaigns? Are you making any headway?

By measuring customer satisfaction with your competitors, both as points on a scale and in terms of the attitudes that support them, you can use measurement strategies offensively to enlarge your market share rather than merely as a defense. Areas of dissatisfaction, lack of satisfaction, or stasis can become the targets for your strategic planning. Not only will the targets announce themselves. Their rank order or susceptibility will also be revealed as well as indications for timing your approach.

Measuring at Headquarters and Division Units

When customers make a considered purchase, it is always a complex process. Multiple decisions are usually involved: Individuals and business managers ask, "Shall I initiate, shall I recommend, shall I decide, shall I try to exert a contrary influence, shall I overrule, shall I go along this time but reassert myself more strongly the next time around? Does my being "satisfied" mean that I am a team player who prefers not to delay a necessary decision unnecessarily; does being "dissatisfied" mean that I am expressing my individuality?"

The Consumer Household as Headquarters

For consumer products makers and service suppliers, the household is their basic satisfaction unit. It is headquarters for the family. It therefore presents a relatively straightforward measurement task. The nature of the product or service itself often preselects the decision maker whose satisfaction determines purchase and use. Some products are so obviously intended for men or women, for adults or teenagers, for general or specific users, that it is simple to focus on the single person who must be satisfied. In many cases, this person is the decision maker, the purchaser, and the user all in one. In other cases, these functions may be divided among a mother and her children, an owner and his pets, or a husband and wife. In still other cases, the concurrence of one household member may be required to motivate a jointly used purchase by the other.

Even when household satisfaction becomes a jointly determined measurement, such as in the cases of family vacations, second-home locations, automobiles, household furnishings, investments, and even some foods, it is never as complex as the measurement of satisfaction with business products and services.

Business Decentralization

In the business environment, there is rarely a single decision maker, even though one manager may, in the final analysis, turn out to be the key decider. Multiple decision making is predetermined in business by the need to ensure the contributions of all interested parties as well as diffusing the blame for them if they go wrong.

A two-part process is required to measure satisfaction with business customers. Even consumer products makers must deal with it, because they relate in a business-to-business mode with their retailers. Part one of the process focuses on a business customer's headquarters operations that command, control, and communicate the policies of the organization. Part two concerns the customer's operating units: divisions or departments that group common businesses, strategic business units (SBUs) that centralize profit-making responsibility, and sales and support offices that execute and implement their operations.

In this diverse complex of interrelationships, you are likely to find as many individual differences as similarities from customer to customer. If you deal with small, entrepreneurial customers, the owner-manager will be the chief determiner of satisfaction. When he is satisfied, his business will be. He is, naturally, subject to influence by the small number of chief operating people he employs. But it is *his* business and, in the last analysis, either he is satisfied or there is no appeal.

If you have a customer base that is composed of larger,

multiproduct customers who generate millions or billions of dollars in revenues each year, a different headquarters situation will challenge your measurement capabilities. Policy-makers and troublemakers abound. Among them, influencers and implementers circulate freely, each expressing his own reactions to doing business with you. In practically every case, no single manager controls, nor wants to control, the corporate satisfaction.

The act of "taking the temperature" at a customer's headquarters is further complicated by the ways and means that the interrelationships of its operating units are carried out. For some aspects of a customer's business, the purchasing manager's satisfaction may be paramount. This will occur whenever you vend mature, commodity products such as office systems for communications and data processing, on the basis of their price and performance. The crux of how satisfactory you are may depend on how elastic you have shown yourself to be in discounting price, making deals or adding premiums: how "easy to do business with" you are.

In other types of sales situations, members of several user groups can become involved. These will be the people who will store and stock your product, train other people to operate and maintain it, endure its downtime, serve its needs for maintenance, finance its first cost and life-cycle operating and maintenance costs, and otherwise work to make it productive at high levels of cost-effectiveness. In addition, you will have to deal with managers of customer business units and sales. They are the people who hear the complaints of their own customers about the contributions you are making to their products and who will have to fulfill warranty and insurance claims that pay for your failures.

How can you tell which of these people can help you grow your business or can subvert your best-laid plans? Each of them has a specific set of values in mind that he or she must receive from you in order to be satisfied. These values are position-specific. In the case of a hospital, for example, the administrator and chief financial officer may be satisfied if your first cost is your last cost and if your return on their investment significantly surpasses their hurdle rate. A director of nursing will have other values. Will her staff be easy to train? Will your product be easy and safe to use, requiring little monitoring and causing no patient problems? The pharmacist will care about your inventory policy to normalize his stock on hand. Any serious dissatisfaction anywhere along the line can work to your detriment.

The same caveat holds true for an industrial customer. The financial officer will typically want a quick payback and high rate of return. The manufacturing manager lives or dies with downtime, scrap rates, and the ability to maintain production schedules without subjecting the business to the catastrophe of recall. The sales manager measures your contribution by how your product adds to his own product's margin or speeds up its sales cycle.

The product manager, running a strategic business unit, is concerned with how you can affect his profits. What is the impact you have on his own customers' satisfaction? More than anything, this may determine his satisfaction with you.

Measuring Users and Distributors

Within the context of customer headquarters and operating units, you must measure the satisfaction of two types of managers. One is *end users*, a term used broadly to include upper-level managers of both headquarters and operations who make policy or decisions about doing business with you. The results they evaluate may range from the financial benefits you provide in terms of cost reduction or increased revenues to the performance benefits that flow from your products and product-related services. The second type is the *middlemen* who manage your customers' distribution channels. They include retail managers in both chains and independent stores, distributors and dealers, and specialists like original equipment manufacturers and value-added resellers known as VARS.

The focus on these two types of managers suggests a basic truth about the measurement of customer satisfaction: Customers tend to see your business as a company principally through the keyhole of your product lines. If they are satisfied with the products you supply and apply to their businesses, they are prepared to see you as a satisfactory company to do business with. You can think of this phenomenon as inferential satisfaction. It is based on "if-then" reasoning: If the products that your company makes are good, then you must be a good company. This type of reasoning drives backwards from what is known— one of your products works in a satisfactory manner—to what is less well known or unknown about how your company works.

Good products, good service, good policies and practices are perceived to be the result of good management. Conversely, products that a customer cannot care highly about are assumed to come from a company that cannot care highly about its customers.

From an end-user's point of view, there are two ways a supplier's product "works." One is the *financial performance* values that a product provides in terms of the improved profits it contributes to a customer's business. The other is its *performance* values. The first criterion measures dollars. The second standard is based on operating specifications. The proof of the operating standards is found in the financial values. How many dollars of cost reduction do the operating features and benefits produce; how many dollars of new revenues do they yield? When end-users express their satisfaction with you, they are essentially playing back their reaction to how much better off you make them appear on their bottom lines.

Middlemen evaluate you in exactly the same manner. They, too, have business units to run. In their case, it is a distribution business of one kind or another. Their criteria for satisfaction are also congregated on their bottom lines. Do your products and trade promotions help them reduce their major variable costs for labor and inventory management? Do you help them increase the turnover on which they depend for their cash flow?

These decisions are functions of two areas of knowledge on your part. How well do you know the internal operations of your customer businesses: Do you know how to affect their costs? How well do you know your customers' customers: Do you know how to stimulate your customers sales to them and to increase their satisfaction with your customers? In this latter category, there is an implicit invitation for you to become partners with your customers who are middlemen. Acting together, you can help them manage satisfaction of their own markets on which the prosperity of both of your businesses depends.

Measuring Work Groups

Small businesses can be measured as if they are single operating units. The executives and function managers are generally one and the same people. Within all customer companies of $5 million or more annual revenues, customer satisfaction should be measured at two levels:

1. *Central Executive Group.* Enterprise-type customer decisionmakers such as chief executive and chief operating officers, chief financial officers, business division or group managers, and staff officers such as purchasing and management information systems or telecommunications managers.

2. *Functional Work Groups.* It is estimated that there are over 10 million functional work groups in American businesses with twenty or more employees. Each group represents a buying unit that can be measured as a "satisfaction cell." There are two types of groups:

- *General Work Groups* such as accounting and finance, strategic planning, sales, advertising and public relations, and customer service.

- *Technical Work Groups* such as R&D, engineering, and manufacturing.

Even though they may work for the same company, members of each of these groups have different values that must be satisfied. What is more, they have different standards of value that determine what is satisfactory and what is not, and different ways of expressing their preferences and aversions. There is no industry-wide or corporate universal satisfaction. Satisfaction is explicitly group-specific, determined by each group's operating requirements and the professional culture of its members.

Analyzing the Measurements

There are four main methods for analyzing measurements of customer satisfaction: Evaluating top-scale positive responses, evaluating bottom-scale negative responses, creating satisfied-dissatisfied ratios, and developing weighted results.

1. *Top-Scale Positives.* By whatever type of scale you choose to measure your "very satisfied" and "satisfied" ratings—the two top categories of measurement—you can combine them into an overall level of satisfaction. A high level of satisfaction exists if the top categories add up to between 85 and 95 percent. Average satisfaction ranks from 70 to 80 percent while anything under 60 percent is low.

2. *Bottom-Scale Negatives.* In similar fashion, you can combine the two lowest bottom-scale negatives to yield an overall level of dissatisfaction. You can expect that your levels of dissatisfaction from adding together your "very dissatisfied" and "dissatisfied" ratings will generally average well below 50 percent if you have a high level of satisfaction and well above 50 percent if your satisfaction level at the top of the scale is low.

3. *Satisfied-Dissatisfied Ratio.* You can make relation-

ships between your positive and negative scores that will highlight your customers' specific areas of concern. A value-to-price relationship that runs 3 to 1 on the positive side correlates with a high level of satisfaction. Your sales presentations need to be improved if they score a 1-to-6 ratio of satisfied-dissatisfied reactions. At 2 to 1, your responsiveness to customer inquiries is good, but not good enough to be competitively dominant.

4. *Weighted Results.* If you assign each response category an arbitrary weighted value, you can illuminate discrepancies between the highs and lows. The scale below shows two forms of weighting for a typical set of classifications.

	FORM A	FORM B
Category	*Weighted* Score	*Weighted* Score
Very satisfied	+2	10
Satisfied	+1	6
Neutral	0	3
Dissatisfied	−1	1
Very dissatisfied	−2	0

At IBM, for example, measurement analysis is fed into the compensation packages of managers who are responsible for customer satisfaction on behalf of their strategic business units. Improvements in satisfaction are rewarded and losses are penalized. Looked at in this way, customer satisfaction is regarded as a bank account into which deposits earn credit and withdrawals are costly.

When specific satisfaction problems are detected by the IBM system, local branch office managers are charged with the responsibility to rectify them. Their compensation system gives them a positive motivation to take remedial action. Their internal control system adds motivation of another kind. As a result, managers at IBM know that it is better all around to assure satisfaction as a steady state than to rush to remedy it when, too late, it shows up as a negative. IBM's customers know, too, that their dissatisfactions trigger responses. When they want attention, they get it. For that reason, they do not take lightly their partnership role in the measurement of their satisfaction.

Strategies like these to satisfy a troubled customer are far from universal. Porsche Cars of North America has its own way of moderating customer complaints. In response to a protest that a dealer had displayed bad faith that resulted in a $3,000 overcharge, Porsche's Customer Service Operations Manager wrote, "We would like you to know that customer satisfaction is vitally important to us." He then told the customer that "the dealer will possibly be filing litigation against you" as a result of the complaint. Nonetheless, he concluded by saying, "on behalf of Porsche Cards of North America, we thank you for taking the time in writing to us."

When you settle on a measurement style to be your own standard, its results can be structured into norms against which you can compare your future scores. This will provide you with benchmarks of what constitutes standard satisfactory performance.

Measurement Methods

The three methods of greatest cost-effectiveness for measuring satisfaction are telephone studies, direct mailings, and a sequential approach that combines telephone, mail, and telephone.

By using the telephone, a sample of up to 500 or more can be interviewed in economical and meaningful fashion. It is best not to identify your company as the sponsor of the research. With the other two methods, identifying yourself as the sponsor is often acceptable. Large-scale mailings directed to multiple segments of 50 each, up to the 500 or so total, frequently result in return rates of 40 to 50 percent. When necessary or desirable, the mailings can be followed up by telephone or, as a more expensive alternative, personal interviews.

The sequential TMT method of telephone-mail-telephone helps to ensure customer understanding of a study's needs, gains superior cooperation and commitment, and acts as a prod to ensure results. Each respondent is first alerted by telephone to the importance of the forthcoming mail survey and, at the same time, is verified as a member of the proper response segment. The personal linkage allows you to go back to the same segment for clarification or supplementary information at a later date.

This is a good way for you to gather together your key respondents into cells for long-term measurement. If a monthly research plan is followed, 10 to 15 cells can be analyzed at one time. On an annual basis, 120 to 150 cells can be interviewed. As your needs change, the number or size of the cells can be expanded or the frequency of your communications with them stepped up.

Quick-Screen Measurement

If you need a finger-on-the pulse type of playback from your customers, you can quick-screen at quarterly intervals. Figure 5 shows a minimal schedule of factors for quick testing. They are adapted from the "must lists" of customers in a cross-section of industries. It is important that they remain minimal in number so that they will always represent the 20 percent of all factors that can influence up to 80 percent of satisfaction. You can add your own industry-specific and customer-specific factors to the minimal schedule in order to make it relevant. But, in doing so, you should keep three caveats in mind:

1. The supplier must always be evaluated on reliability, not likeability or admirability.
2. The products must always be evaluated on adequacy with which they deliver the operating benefits of your technology. Adequacy is sufficient; supremacy

FIGURE 5. FACTORS FOR QUICK-SCREEN MEASUREMENT.

Customer's Name _____

Customer's Business Function _____

SUPPLIER VALUES

	POOR									*EXCELLENT*

Reliability in delivering on promises

Deliver what they promise	1	2	3	4	5	6	7	8	9	10
Deliver when they promise	1	2	3	4	5	6	7	8	9	10

Reliability in making good

Stand behind their promises	1	2	3	4	5	6	7	8	9	10
Repair or replace what they sell	1	2	3	4	5	6	7	8	9	10
Operate on a no-fault basis	1	2	3	4	5	6	7	8	9	10
Make their top people available	1	2	3	4	5	6	7	8	9	10

PRODUCT VALUES

	1	2	3	4	5	6	7	8	9	10
Adequate technology	1	2	3	4	5	6	7	8	9	10
Adequate flexibility for expansion and upgrading to postpone obsolescence	1	2	3	4	5	6	7	8	9	10
Pays back our investment in conformity to our hurdle rate	1	2	3	4	5	6	7	8	9	10
Earns maximum return on our investment	1	2	3	4	5	6	7	8	9	10
Can be leased or rented to avoid balance-sheet commitment	1	2	3	4	5	6	7	8	9	10

SALES AND PRODUCT-RELATED SERVICE VALUES

	1	2	3	4	5	6	7	8	9	10
Sell to us on the basis of reducing our costs	1	2	3	4	5	6	7	8	9	10
Sell to us on the basis of increasing our sales revenues	1	2	3	4	5	6	7	8	9	10
Know our business best	1	2	3	4	5	6	7	8	9	10
Work as partners with our people	1	2	3	4	5	6	7	8	9	10
Know their own business and how to apply their capabilities to our business to solve our problems	1	2	3	4	5	6	7	8	9	10
Train our people	1	2	3	4	5	6	7	8	9	10
Include top-notch technical representatives	1	2	3	4	5	6	7	8	9	10

is not required. Your products do not have to be innovative or leading-edge to maximize satisfaction.
3. Sales and product-related services must always be evaluated in terms of relevance to your customer's businesses and your ability to implement the application of your expertise to improve them.

Customer Satisfaction Index

BSI and The Wellspring Group have created a multidimensional customer satisfaction index that can calculate the impact of each form of added value on customer satisfaction. The index contains two types of information:

- *Plus-Side Values,* which account for a supplier's ability to add value
- *Minus-Side Values,* which account for lost values or a lost opportunity to add value.

These aspects of the index are shown in Figure 6. Findings derived from the index can be aggregated by market segment as well as by individual customer, allowing comprehensive market calculations to be made.

The Common Denominator: People

These caveats may challenge your preconceptions of what "must be" the basis for customer satisfaction and therefore ought to be measured. Yet time after time, in industry after industry, the best liked and most admired company can be found among the minimal satisfiers; the most innovative product based on the highest technology does not automatically yield maximum satisfaction; and the people who contribute the most to satisfaction are consultative implementers who partner closely and continuingly with their customers.

This is not to say that a supplier cannot be well liked or

FIGURE 6. CUSTOMER SATISFACTION INDEX.

PLUS-SIDE VALUES

      ABILITY TO ADD VALUE   *CUSTOMER EVALUATION*

      (1) Reduced Costs   _____ (40%)

      (2) Increased Sales   _____ (40%)

      (3) Other:

          _____   _____

                                                  (20%)

          _____   _____

MINUS-SIDE VALUES

      INABILITY TO ADD VALUE   *CUSTOMER EVALUATION*

      (1) Costs Not Reduced

          or Costs Increased   _____ *(40%)*

      (2) Sales Not Increased

          or Sales Lost   _____ *(40%)*

      (3) Other:

          _____   _____ *(20%)*

          _____   _____

admired and still be his industry's satisfier. It will depend on what he is liked or admired *for*. If he is positioned as ethical, that is a reliability factor. If he meets obligations and regularly makes his top people available to customers, these are also reliability factors. But if his people are just "nice folks" to do business with, they will probably be considered to be just as nice not to do business with.

Similarly, nothing precludes a leading-edge product from contributing to maximum satisfaction. But a product does not need to possess innovative technology in order to do so. Whether it does or not, the essential measurement is that its contribution must be adequate— and in many cases "adequate" may be very high indeed— to help improve a customer's performance. Leading-edge products, on other hand, often prove to be "bleeding edge" in terms of their unsatisfactory costs.

Where the best is a necessity is in the area of a supplier's people, especially those who interface with customers. Given sophisticated managers and adequate products, superior people provide the third ingredient in the trinity required for maximum customer satisfaction. They are the ones who carry the standard of your company's reliability to the field. They are also the people who put your products to work in the most cost-effective manner within their customers' business functions, train the customer's people to bring out their full contribution, and form partnerships with the customer's managers.

If there is a magic formula for maximizing customer satisfaction, it is this: *Make your company reliable. Make your products adequate. Make your product implementers the best.*

An examination of the three major contributors to customer satisfaction reveals their common denominator. Each is dependent on the performance of *your people*. The supplier's values come from your people's knowledge about the customer and their abilities in applying it. A product's values come from your people's engineering and manufacturing knowledge and their ability to implement it in the customer's operations.

Customer satisfaction can now be seen for what it is: *Your people satisfying your customer's people.* It is a people-to-people process because it is people who deliver and sustain satisfaction, not corporations. Products alone do not satisfy; they are dependent on how well they are installed in a customer's functions and processes. They must be properly prescribed, properly implemented, and properly monitored. Sales and service by themselves do not satisfy; they are dependent on how well sales and service people act as partners with their counterparts in the customer's business. In every case, satisfaction is people-dependent. When your customers are satisfied with you, it is your people they are satisfied with.

When you measure customer satisfaction, you are essentially measuring the values that your people possess for customer people. The "they" whose contributions you evaluate are not corporate entities. Neither are they product entities. They are your people, and you will be measuring them in two ways: how they perform in partnership with your customer's people and how they perform in competition with your rivals for the right to command exclusivity in their partnerships. Because it is the customer's privilege to grant partnerships and to keep them exclusive, all of your efforts to measure customer satisfaction will be a test of *how well you are denying customers the privilege of dissatisfaction with you.* Only monopolists can ignore this rule with impunity.

In setting up your measurement scales, you need to ask, "What are the values our people must deliver to their customer's people?" The customers' "must list" will give you the answer.

Then you need to ask a second question: "How well are our people enhancing each customer's values?" Your answer will yield your customer's value-to-price perception of his relationship with you. For him, it will determine his value expressed as the return he receives from his investment with you. For you, it will determine your price expressed as the customer's investment. Unless your measurements reveal high value in relation to your price, your margins will be at risk.

Measuring Your People's Performance

To test how well your people are delivering customer values, you must test both absolute and comparative values—your own contributions first and then how they stack up comparatively against your competitors' contributions.

When you test absolute values, you will need to seek out superlative responses that affirm your values to be the *best*. When you test competitively, you will need to seek out comparative responses that affirm your values to be *better*. You will then be able to match your absolute values against each of your competitor's values. In these ways, you will know where you stand.

American Express (Amex) is a company that asks the right questions. To answer the question "What are the values we must deliver?" Amex has identified 180 measurable criteria for assessing its customers' satisfaction. High on the list are the time it takes to replace lost credit cards or to respond to billing inquiries. For each criterion on its "must list", Amex has established a performance standard. Lost cards must be replaced within two days and customers must have their billing inquiries answered by the tenth day.

Other companies impose their own "must lists" on their suppliers. The Kroger Company, a nationwide grocery, drug, and convenience store chain, scores suppliers on their timing of deliveries. This is a major aspect of Kroger's cost of doing business. If goods are sent in to Kroger's warehouses too soon, inventory costs go up. Kroger also incurs an additional opportunity cost if it has to pay for the goods before they can be resold, using its own money instead of cash flow. A supplier who costs Kroger money in these ways gets a low grade. If he does not improve to

Kroger's satisfaction, Kroger will switch to another supplier.

Many companies are in businesses whose customers depend on the continuity of production to survive. These companies have discovered that replacing a malfunctioning part is generally more satisfactory to a customer than trying to repair it. It takes less time and it generally solves the problem the first time. These companies keep a registry that stores the specifications of each customer's equipment. They use airborne express services to ship out replacements from a central warehouse. Overnight, the customer is back in business.

One company that does this is Auto Shack, a medium-size operator of about 400 automobile parts stores in fifteen states. Its policy is to "save the sale" through customer satisfaction. Even when one of its stores is out of stock on a part, Auto Shack wants to keep a customer from going to a competitor. Yet a typical store cannot carry all of Auto Shack's 30,000 parts.

To solve the problem, Auto Shack maintains a computerized warehouse that holds every part and has a direct telecommunications link to each retail store. This gives Auto Shack three options when a part is needed: Get the part from a nearby store or ship it overnight from either the warehouse or the vendor. Anything from an engine to a set of spark plugs can be in a customer's hands no later than the next day, seven days a week. In almost every case, this satisfies the customer and also satisfies Auto Shack's objective to save the sale.

Ensuring Your People's Reliability

It is true for all customers in all industries that the single most important criterion of satisfaction in dealing with a supplier is his *reliability*. Not only must his products and services perform. The supplier as a corporate person must perform too. He must deliver what he promises by the time he has promised it. He must be dependable to make things go right or to fix them when they go wrong. His motto, whether stated or implicit in how he conducts himself, must be "The customer is always right." Only when the customer is always right is a supplier always satisfactory.

It is important to understand what the customer is always right about. Every supplier knows customers who are inept, inert as partners, incompetent, and, on top of everything, imperious. Yet they must always be right if you are going to satisfy them. What makes them right? They are right to expect that they will enhance their business operations or personal life styles by engaging you. When they do not, or when they fall short of the degree of enhancement they expect, they are right to register their dissatisfaction with you. That is strike one. If you deflect the blame back onto them, or ignore their disappointment, that is strike two. If a competitor can bring those customers the enhancement they originally sought from you or, in concert with them, agree that the displacement of blame onto you is fair, that is strike three. You will be out.

Reliability is the sine qua non of customer satisfaction. It will be reflected in your superior grades to questions like these about your business:

- Is the supplier reliable? Does he deliver what he promises?
- Does he deliver it on time?
- Does he stand out in dependability—can you count on him?
- If there is a mix-up or a foul-up, does he stand behind his initial promise and make it good?
- No matter whose fault it is, when you get into a tight squeeze can you rely on him to come to the rescue and find fault later?
- When you include him in your plans, can you sleep well at night?

In order to be the reliability leader, which means that your level of reliability sets the standard for your industry, reliability must be your corporate compulsion. You must do everything with 100 percent assurance of your customers' satisfaction. You must do nothing without this assurance.

This requires you to have a process for reliability assurance. The process must be corporatewide, ingrained in every one of your managers in every function. It must consist of checks and balances, a system of controls that will mediate two conflicting motivations:

1. To satisfy the customer at all costs, which leads to cutting corners, moving up deadlines, fudging specifications, and all the other attributes of overcommitment.
2. To satisfy the customer at low cost, which leads to cutting corners, moving up deadlines, fudging specifications, and all the other attributes of undercommitment.

The motivation in the first instance may be praiseworthy. But the end result is just as destructive of customer satisfaction as the less praiseworthy motivation in the second instance. Yet both of these aberrations grow out of the same situation—recognition of the transcendent importance of customer satisfaction.

There are two measurements that you can use to test for reliability. The first is a *premeasurement*. It is conducted internally by each of your managers asking the screening question, is what I am doing contributing to maximum customer satisfaction? When your R&D, engineering, and manufacturing managers ask this question of themselves and their people, more satisfactory products result. When your marketing managers ask this question, better promotions result. Nothing that elicits a negative answer should ever leave your corporate premises.

Premeasurements, honestly and continually carried out, should predict the results of the *postmeasurements* you will then make in the market itself. Postmeasures tell how well premeasurement is working. They also act as invaluable feedback to bring your internal measurement process more fully in line with the customer's real world.

Evaluating the Competition

Competition for your customers' satisfaction is a race that has only one winner. He will be found at the high-satisfaction end of the measurement scale. All others, even if they come in second, will be effectively last. Number Two may find it easier to rationalize his position, but, from a practical standpoint, he is little better off than the supplier who is dead last. There is only one number to be and that is Number One. He will be the industry standard-setter. As long as his performance sets the norms of satisfaction, everyone else must try to play catch-up and overtake him. To be "just as good as" is not the same as "better than." Therefore, "just as good as" will never be quite good enough.

Competitors can affect your customers' satisfaction with you in three ways:

1. If they are less satisfying than you are, your competitors can act as inadvertent suppliers of customers to you.
2. If they are more satisfying than you are, your competitors can act as consumers of your customers by "eating your lunch."
3. If they are equally satisfying, your competitors can act to obscure your differentiation and thereby accelerate your loss of satisfaction supremacy.

The competitor who is more satisfactory than you are is your immediate challenge. The competitor who equals you is your constant peril. He will blunt your distinctiveness while he is parallel to you, share your advantages even if they do not properly accrue to him, and leave you diminished if he surpasses you.

In industries where strategic alliances with a small

number of suppliers is becoming the rule, to be Number Three or worse is to be almost out of the running. To be tied for Number Two or to be Number Three is often to be reduced to the status of an also-ran from the outset.

The also-ran position of a competitor makes him an unwilling supplier of customers for you by virtue of providing lesser satisfaction to them than you do. In this way, the competitor supplements your own strategies for customer development without making demands on your funds or other resources. This can be thought of as "putting a competitor to work for us." In hotly contested markets, you will probably have no choice. If you do not position your competitors as suppliers of customers, they will do it to you.

Your ability to convert a competitor into a supplier depends on how much better you are at satisfying customers. At the point where you pass breakeven—where you and a competitor are no longer perceived as equal in providing satisfaction, as Figure 7 shows—the competitor starts to act as your supplier of customers.

Each customer's "must list" is your crucial resource. One you know it, you can begin to take a position on it alongside your major competitors. Because it is the customer's yardstick of the essential elements of his satisfaction, it is the only scale that matters. It says that customer satisfaction is not what you think it is. Nor is it what you would like it to be. *Satisfaction is what the customer says it is*.

The "satisfactors" on every customer's "must list" are both industry-dependent and customer-specific. Each industry has some exclusive factors of its own or ranks similar factors differently. The same is true of individual customers. Nevertheless, these are only 20 percent of the total. The 80 percent are remarkably consistent across industry and customer lines. From this mix, you will have to find the smallest number of factors that act to swing customer preferences. These will be the hinges that convert competitors into your suppliers—or you into theirs.

FIGURE 7. COMPETITOR CONVERSION CURVE.

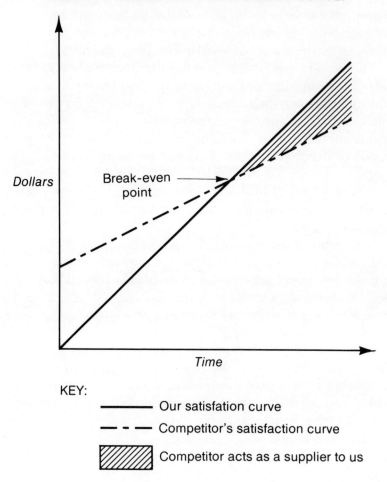

Beating the Ratings Lag

Standard measurements of customer satisfaction that are taken only on an annual basis often cannot be acted on for as long as thirty-six to forty-eight months. As a result, customer defections and competitive inroads leading to market decline may already have become irreversible by the time an alarm has sounded and relief can be implemented. Even if doing too little can be avoided, it will still be too late. Many problems will have matured for as long as a year or two. The chance for timely solutions, or even sincere apologies, will have vanished.

Figure 8 shows the problem. In any given year, referred to as Year One, market slide and competitive share-building may begin among a small number of dissatisfied customers. Nonetheless, Year Two satisfaction ratings can remain high even though sales show an early warning sign of a drop. Although market share has started to erode, it will not be until Year Three that the annual satisfaction measurement can reflect its cause and extent. In most companies, it will take until Year Four to agree on a corrective satisfaction program.

This argues for a quarterly "Customer Needs Challenge" of the customers who are your growings and growables. The BSI-Wellspring approach is shown in Figure 6.

FIGURE 8. THE RATINGS LAG.

Each quarterly study can be as small as ten customers a month, totaling thirty a quarter. This is a low price to pay to condense reaction time by as much as three years.

Putting Measurement Figures to Work

Customer satisfaction is dynamic. It is a transient quality, fluctuating over time with rises and falls that can be caused as much by your constancy when change is required as by your changes when consistency is necessary. No customer is satisfied once and for all time. Nor are customers likely to be universally satisfied at the same level of satisfaction across a broad spectrum of values. This is because satisfaction is a composite of values, a resolution of positive and negative factors that can net out today different from tommorow. You need to do nothing to cause it to vary. Indeed, your very inaction may be sufficient cause.

Satisfaction is a measurement taken at a point in time. Its position can be measured by freezing the point. By plotting its motion and tracking its progress, you can develop its trend. Satisfaction with you as a whole can be assayed, as can its components. When they are compared with the positions and trends of your competitors, rankings can be made of the current state of rivalry for "share of satisfaction" in your industry.

Each of your rivals is fighting for a larger share of the pie called customer satisfaction. Your slice represents a share of your market's conviction that *it must buy from you, that it must buy only from you, and that it must buy from you again.* This conviction can be referred to as a "must buy." It causes your customers to say "I have to" when they are asked, "Why do you do business with them?" What they mean by this, of course, is that they perceive they have no choice if they want to be satisfied at the level you have standardized.

Once you know your current score as a customer satisfier, you can compare it with your score at the last measurement point to detect its trend and contrast it with the score of your competitors; then you can make strategy. You will be able to do for yourself exactly what you can do to satisfy your customers: Use your own norms as the base line for the application of your capabilities. If your score is low or is moving down, you will have to apply remedial strategies to become competitive again. If your score is high or is moving up, you will have to apply your current strategies with renewed vigor in order to maintain your momentum.

If your score is stable, you will have to hurry to apply growth strategies before your stability degenerates into decline. Three types of products may call for one or more growth strategies: renovated products, new products, and mature products.

Renovated Products

In spite of general customer satisfaction with one of your products, you may discover that its score is qualified by a single area of dissatisfaction or a related complex of small dissatisfactions. This is a signal for you to renovate the product to bring it back to competitive strength. The measurement process will tell you the specific areas you need to attend to as well as the amount and type of enhancements to features or benefits that are required.

New Products

An increasing score for a competitor's product accompanied by a stable or declining score for your own product is a signal for you to innovate. If you are losing satisfaction in only one or a few benefits, marginal renovations may suffice. But if your product is becoming generally noncompetitive, a new product may be called for. New products will also call themselves to your attention when there is a high pervasive level of general dissatisfaction with all competitive offerings in a category, including your own.

Mature Products

A long-term flatness or precipitous decline in a mature product's score is a signal to consider phasing it out. The signal will be especially strong if satisfaction is similarly declining for your competitors. The market may be telling you that it has outgrown the entire product category or that the product has become a commodity that provides basic utility but is easily replicated. Since no supplier can establish sufficient preference in this type of market to command margins conducive to high profit, phase-out or divestment may be the most cost-effective growth strategy.

The Historical Secret

When customer satisfaction is looked at in historical perspective, its foundation becomes clear. In earlier decades, customer–supplier relationships were generally rated as being more satisfactory by both parties. The satisfaction levels of a majority of relationships were uniformly high and showed impressive staying power; they endured, with few ups and downs of significance. In retrospect, the customer and supplier people who managed these relationships can put their fingers on why they believe customer satisfaction was once easier to achieve and maintain.

Companies were smaller then. People knew each other better, and they compiled data bases on customer needs and supplier capabilities from firsthand experiences. With eased access, multiple partnering was more naturally accomplished. Management hierarchies were smaller, so all the major players were well known to each other and could be brought into the planning, decision-making, and implementation loops. Specific responsibility for maintaining customer satisfaction was the domain of the supplier's managers who acted as, and were sometimes referred to as, "customer's men." The customer's man was available 24 hours a day, seven days a week. Similarly, the customer was available to him. Data flowed freely. There were few surprises.

The secret of customer satisfaction was then, as it is now, vested in a supplier's people working intimately with the customer's people, sharing information, tracking results, and always implementing improvements in the customer's business. The supplier's ability to satisfy is a function of "being there," resident in the customer's operations, learning the source of his problems and opportunities as they occur and generating a steady stream of proposals to solve the problems and capture the opportunities. It is a function of recognizing the special nature of each customer's business and dedicating the best people to be his partners—best because they know the customer best and are the best able to improve his profits and productivity.

As companies have grown, as customer lists have multiplied in the search for an ever-increasing market share, and as the vending approach to selling has more and more emphasized the quick hit, the features-and-benefits sales pitch, and service only on demand, the personal touch has weakened in many relationships. Without it, suppliers are virtually interchangeable in most industries. As their technologies cyclically net out at parity, their products become homogenized and the premium falls more and more heavily on their people.

Businesses that understand satisfaction in the context of today's needs are organizing themselves into small units that replicate history in their dedication to specific customers. They are staffing each business unit with customer specialists whose mission is to improve the profit contribution of specific customer operations. As a result, profit-improvement partnerships are replacing buy-and-sell relationships, consultative selling is replacing vendor selling, and the mission of improving customer profits is replacing moving goods as the major measurement of success.

4

Marketing Customer Satisfaction

The ability to satisfy a customer—to satisfy him enough to sell him initially in spite of fierce competition and to keep him satisfied thereafter—is the highest business skill.

Because customers are the source of your business, providing the source of needs that call forth your benefits and the source of your profits from providing them, they are your most precious resource. You can never own them. Nor can you control them. You can only satisfy them if you can attract them in the first place and hold onto them as they, and you, grow. It stands to reason, therefore, that the men and women in your business who have the skills to satisfy customers are the most important people in your employ. Everyone else should be committed to their support.

Your company's mission statement should dedicate the

business to the maximum satisfaction of your core customers. Every aspect of the organization and operation of the business should be conducive to maximum customer satisfaction. Your policies, products and value-to-price relationships should each be devised with one preeminent objective in mind: Is this the best way to maximize the satisfaction of our core customers? If not, what can possibly justify it? Looked at in this way, total customer satisfaction must become the master criterion for everything your business makes and markets.

If you are your industry's best satisfier, there is nothing more important for you to market. Existing customers will be comforted by the reinforcement that this knowledge adds to their partnerships with you. Prospective customers will be attracted. Competitors, unable to counterclaim meaningfully, will be disadvantaged in the most vulnerable area of their positioning. They will have nothing to sell that compares.

What does it mean to be "the best satisfier?" It means to satisfy best a market's most important needs and to seriously dissatisfy none of the others.

Marketing the Ability to Satisfy

For the purpose of marketing, it would be highly unsatisfactory for you to say, "We satisfy best." While it would defy modesty and dilute credibility, its worst impact would be on its effectiveness. Only a satisfied customer can credibly attest to your ability to satisfy. The marketing message must therefore revolve around a testimonial theme of "I am satisfied best," proclaiming the satisfaction of your customers, by your customers, and for your customers.

Your ability to satisfy is commendable, but it is not marketable. Only your achievements are marketable. A customer's satisfaction is your sole marketing platform. One satisfied customer's case history is worth a thousand of your own self-serving claims.

Suppliers who make customer satisfaction their most important product have no choice but to practice true marketing—that is, to allow everything they do in front of customers to be driven by the market. Their answer to the question, "What is the most important thing we can say about ourselves?" is *"nothing."* The only important things are those said by customers, not about their supplier but about themselves after being enhanced by the supplier.

Without things like these to say, suppliers must satisfy themselves with talk about their own products and processes. As a result, they pseudo-market. Many of them call it serving their market's needs to be informed, to make wise choices based on information, and to differentiate themselves competitively from other vendors by "telling them why they should do business with us." But if any service is performed, it is most likely self-service.

True marketing of customer satisfaction is a three part system:

1. The creation and proclamation of your *norms* as representing the industry norms for satisfaction in each key area of customer needs.
2. The publication of *testimonial case histories* that show how customers have been able to achieve your norms by working with you.
3. Your *proposals* to approach the norms for specific customers.

Marketing From Norms

If you control the norms of your customer's industry you control the industry. You become its de facto leader, cornering the most crucial knowledge an industry must possess about itself—the optimal operating values for its vital processes. Your norms tell an industry's participants how their major business functions should be performing. The performance values represented by your norms are the best values that are cost-effective to achieve. By inference, your norms represent you as being the most cost-effective partner to work with.

"How much of a scrap rate should we tolerate for a start-up operation?" a manufacturer asks. IBM is the keeper of the norms. "How much deviation from specifications should be allowed during a production run?" an automobile maker asks. Honda is the keeper of the norms. IBM's ability to normalize manufacturing productivity and Honda's ability to normalize quality are legendary. Many manufacturers specify "IBM or equal" for their plant automation partners. Even GM specifies "Honda or equal."

When you represent the performance standard that your customers know they should achieve—and that they must achieve in order to remain competitive—you have taken the first step in the marketing process. You have defined a common objective with your customers. For their part, customers want to attain the norm or maintain it if they are already performing at the normative level. You are in the position of wanting to help them attain or maintain it. The basis for partnership is firmly in place.

Marketing based on norms is visibly different from vendor marketing where there is no mutual objective. The vendor wants to transfer his product, moving it out of his inventory into the inventory of his customers. His customers do not typically want the vendor's product at the vendor's price. They certainly do not want the added inventory. But the vendor who does not possess his customer's norms, and therefore cannot market from them, has only his product's performance and price to sell. As a result, his relations with customers are far more likely to be adversarial than partnerships.

Few customers can afford to walk away from the chance to improve their performance according to norms. Only a business that is on a roll, exceeding the high end of the norms by a significant margin, can justify a temporary aloofness. For the rest, norms represent necessary values.

The Double Meaning
of Customer Performance

In the world of norms, the concept of customer performance has a double meaning. In the first instance, it means operating performance. This measures the *productivity* of men and machinery: How many man-hours are required to produce each product unit; how many pounds or tons or gallons or barrels are produced each day; or how many hours of downtime are subtracted from production each month. It also measures the *quality* of productivity. This refers to how many units of scrap are produced in comparison to marketable products, how many finished units must be finally rejected, how many are returned or must be repaired or replaced under warranty.

Because your customers' performance either does or does not conform to a given set of specifications, the majority of operating norms are objective and readily quantifiable. You can say to a customer that the norm for downtime in your type of operation is between ten and fifteen hours per month. How do you compare? If your answer is higher than fifteen, you are incurring unnecessary production losses from downtime. A small number of operating norms are more subjective, which means that they must feel right, smell right, sound right, and look right—as well as work right—in order to be normative. This is the case with many products sold to individual customers.

In the second instance, the concept of customer performance has a *financial* meaning. This measures a different kind of productivity; namely, the return that a customer receives for every dollar he invests in an operation or activity. The *productivity of money* is measured differently from the *productivity of men and machinery*. It is every bit as quantifiable, but the unit of evaluation is dollars, not products: How many dollars are required to produce each product unit and how many dollars does downtime add to costs and subtract from revenues each month? It also measures the *quality* of investment. This refers to how many dollars fail to yield a positive return, how many investments must be written off or written down, and how much opportunity cost is incurred in comparison with other options for the same investment.

Financial Performance Criteria

In the same way that your customers have specifications for operating performance, they also have financial performance criteria. Every investment they approve must surpass a minimum "hurdle rate" of return, below which it will be considered to be unproductive. Customer investments also have time standards for how long it takes to reach payback, how long before positive cash flow begins, how long a superior rate of return will continue, and how superior it must be to alternative investments.

Each financial norm is objective and therefore readily quantifiable. You can say to a customer, "Based on a sales cycle of thirteen weeks that typically involves three calls, the industry norm for the cost of a sale of a product system like yours is $10,000. How do you compare? If your sales cost is more than $10,000, you are incurring unnecessary selling expenses."

Operating norms and financial norms go hand in hand. No process or activity of a customer can be quantified without reference to both of them. Financial norms are, in a sense, proof of the operating norms; that is, they reveal just how productive a customer operation really is by measuring the number of dollars it throws off, either in costs or revenues, compared with the number of time and material units. Very often you will find that a customer will be satisfied with his operating performance. He will not perceive any major discrepancies between the way it functions and the way he thinks it should. He will be reluctant to analyze it, let alone tamper with it, justifying his reticence with the adage, "Don't fix it if it ain't broke." But when you and he audit the financial results of his operations and their departure from the cost or revenue norms that you can deliver, a process that "ain't broke" may suddenly seem able to benefit from repair and restoration.

Norms challenge your customer's complacency about what works. They stimulate urgency where there has been none, either because other hot spots have required more attention or because no credible way of assessing an operation has heretofore been available. Many customers have no awareness that operations on which they depend can be standardized—that is, that normative standards exist for them or that there are cost-effective ways of obtaining them. It is easy for them to believe that "we have good people" and that "they are doing an acceptable job." By marketing from norms, you can offer to make a customer's good people even better and elevate their currently acceptable performance to a level of superiority.

What if the norms for the customer's industry are someone else's? Can you still use them? If you are in the automobile business and you market upscale cars, Mercedes-Benz confronts you as the industry leader in many categories of price and performance. If the Mercedes 190 is the standard of value in its class, why would you buy Ford's Merkur Scorpio? Ford thinks it has a better chance if it guarantees the trade-in value of used Scorpios to be the same as Mercedes' trade-in value. In the same way, Cadillac has guaranteed the resale of its Allante to the value of the Mercedes 560 SL. If Allante sells for less than Mercedes' norm, Cadillac will satisfy its customer by making up the difference.

Marketing From Testimonials

If your norms are perceived as ideals rather than realistically attainable results, they risk being considered ephemeral. Most customers will admit that they *could* do better. But *should* they? After all, improving performance for the sake of improved performance alone is an unappealing business decision. There are always many pressing uses for corporate funds. Unless an operation is producing catastrophic results, there is really only one compelling reason for a customer to invest in approaching a norm: It must be competitively advantageous, either to stay even, to pull up, or to move ahead. When you say to a customer that he should be closer to the norm, you are saying that he should be closer to taking, regaining, or holding a competitive advantage.

The best way for you to dramatize the fact that there is a competitive advantage to making an operation more normative is to show a customer giving testimony to enjoying the advantage. This has two insuperable benefits. It creates *comfort* by assuring other customers that it can be done, that your norm is truly attainable. It also creates *urgency* by showing one competitor moving away from the rest of the field: Your norm is an enhancement that can endow a company with industry leadership through either a lower cost or improved profits from new earnings.

Case histories of customers enjoying the "advantage of the norm" are miniature detective stories. They start with your solution—the new advantage made possible by achieving your norm—backtrack through the improvements in the customer's processes that were necessary to achieve it, and then compare the new advantage to the situation at the start. The difference between the "after" and the "before" is the value added to the customer by your norm.

In case histories like these, customers testify on your behalf. They make you credible in ways that you, saying the same things, could not. They also serve as identifiable role models for other customers who want to emulate them so as to equal or surpass their achievements. Customers identify with other customers, especially those in their own industry or those who share common processes, problems, or markets. When a satisfied customer provides a credible reference for you, he contributes the ultimate reward for satisfaction: the repute that opens the door for you to satisfy again. The following three examples of case histories on behalf of IBM illustrate the effectiveness of this method.

- Black & Decker is a testifier for IBM. The U.S. Power Tools Division is a satisfied customer as a result of gaining $15 million in sales through an IBM data base system. The system increases the order fill rate—the percentage of orders filled immediately—and in this way reduces sales lost because merchandise is unavailable. If you have a business that markets several thousand products like Black & Decker, you will find their experience a credible reference for doing business with IBM in a way that gives significant customer satisfaction.
- Another satisfied customer of IBM is Heinz U.S.A. Their satisfaction comes from saving $200,000 because they were able to increase the productivity of their order entering process by 75 percent. As with Black & Decker, the satisfaction at Heinz is matched by the satisfaction of Heinz customers who get faster and more accurate response to their orders.
- Satisfaction has other ramifications as well. With Timex, IBM was able to reduce inventories of some of the billions of parts the watchmaker requires for is worldwide production and sales. The resulting economies of more than half a million dollars are satisfying not only to the company, but to Timex's shareholders as well.

Who can identify with Black & Decker's satisfaction? Other power tool manufacturers, other manufacturers of complex products that require relatively long manufacturing lead times, other makers of multiproduct lines of business, and other companies that have a problem in matching their production to demand.

Who can identify with Heinz, U.S.A.? Other packaged foods processors, other companies that need to link multiple customer service centers and factories all across the country, and other companies that need to improve their customer service.

Who can identify with Timex? Other manufacturers and assemblers who have multiple production centers on several continents, other companies that handle billions of parts, and other companies that are undergoing rapid global growth yet must maintain close coordination of the various parts of their businesses and accurate determination of the most attractive options.

Marketing From Proposals

The proposal is your invitation to customers to join your norm. It says, in effect, "We have shown you what the norm is; other customers have testified to its attainability and value; now here is the most cost-effective way for you, in partnership with us, to attain a similar value for your own operation."

In proposing to make a customer operation or activity perform in a more satisfactory manner, both as a producer of marketable output and bankable dollars, you should follow a logical, sequential argument composed of the following three parts:

1. *A snapshot of the customer's operation now.* You must capture the essential facts of the customer's operating and financial productivity, in both words and numbers. What is unsatisfactory? What is satisfactory and must be maintained or improved? In each case, what are the operating performance and dollar values involved? How much of them represent unnecessary direct costs; how much are opportunity costs that can be reclaimed?

2. *A moving picture of the customer's operation in the near future.* You must project the improved values that can accrue to the customer in both his operating and financial productivity. How much will the dollar value of productivity increase? When will its benefits first flow? How long will they go on? What investment will be required and what rate of return will it yield? How much of the return will be composed of recaptured costs? How much will be new revenues? What will this more satisfactory scenario look like in cumulative dollars and industry position on an annual basis, showing progress year by year?

3. Proof that the improved satisfaction can be cost-effectively achieved. You must be prepared to document where, when, and how the customer's altered productivity can occur: In what components of the customer's operations, at what time, for how long, and how will the costs be reduced or the revenues increased? Where will improved performance come from? In what dollar values? What will each invested dollar contribute? When will the improvements become self-financing, requiring no further investment of new funds?

This three-part procedure can be summarized as *problem, promise* and *proof.* Through the proposal process, you take on the role of provider of increased satisfaction, drawing a baseline where satisfaction initially stands and then undertaking to elevate it. Your proposition is stipulated in the second part of the proposal. Its value is determined by comparing it with the proposal's first part. In the third part, its value is documented. In short, the rank order of the elements says to the customer, "Here is where you are, here is where we can get you to be in partnership with us, and here is how you can be sure in advance."

Achieving "Good Enoughness"

Quality is always a compromise between what can be maximized technologically and what is optimal to a market. Maximization is an engineering standard. Optimal quality is determined in the marketplace. Only customers can say what it is. Where a supplier's maximum is perceived by customers as suboptimal, there is no market. Where the customer's standard is submaximal but a supplier builds a product to maximum standards anyway, there may be no profit. The costs of maximization may absorb earnings. The customer will not pay for them. The savings from marketing only the optimal solution represent the added value of market research.

The optimal solution is the benefit that is "good enough" to maximize satisfaction. This rarely requires a maximum benefit or maximum stretch of technology to produce. To go beyond the optimal is to provide unnecessary values that add to cost and to price.

"Good enough" means what it says. It does not have to be better. A need that is fulfilled at the "good enough" level does not benefit by being overfulfilled. A problem that is solved does not have to be oversolved. The best solution is the one that works at a customer's desired or required level of performance, that does it the first time and every time thereafter. To go beyond that creates "more-than-enoughness." If it must be paid for without yielding a commensurate return, it will be dissatisfying to the user no matter how satisfying it may be to the engineer who made a breakthrough or pushed back a frontier.

"Good enough" is rarely good enough, however, when it is prejudicially determined by a supplier rather than by his customers. This is management arrogance at its worst. It comes from the belief that quality can be engineered in instead of having to be contracted out to customers. If customer satisfaction is going to be built in, the satisfaction process must flow from the outside; from the markets that are the source of needs to the managers who must satisfy them.

Quality is not an ephemeral concept. It is always a measurable standard. Its relationship to customer satisfaction is one-to-one. Anything that falls short of optimal satisfaction is an invitation to market loss. Increased warranty costs and reduced sales inevitably follow, along with negative effects on reputation that suppress sales even further. Until satisfaction can be brought back to the optimal level, the downward spiral of depressed revenues and increased costs feeds on itself until profits, in the end, are consumed.

Proving Satisfaction in Advance

Throughout the proposal process, it is imperative that the customer is not asked to make a purchase. You must invite him, instead, to make himself more satisfied. The result of accepting your proposal should not be seen as a sale. Instead, the result must be positioned as an enhanced customer operation whose performance can contribute measurably greater satisfaction. The operation will work better. It will also be a better money-maker.

The purpose of the proposal is to prove customer satisfaction in advance—to prove before the proposal is implemented that satisfaction will occur as you propose. The customer must not be asked to speculate. He must not be put in a position of taking the risk that satisfaction may not occur, or that it may not occur in the amount promised, or on time. The proposal establishes a climate of confidence by demonstrating on paper exactly what will happen inside the customer's operation or activity just as if it were a trial run. Here are the values that will be affected, the proposal says. These are the changes in your values that will result. These are the investments you must make and these are their returns.

A proposal to improve customer satisfaction is a rehearsal for your customer partnership to get its act together before the first bolt is fastened, the first shelf stocked, or the first invoice delivered. The challenge of such a proposal is twofold:

1. What is the minimal amount of change that the customer needs to undertake?
2. What is the maximum amount of gain that can come from it?

Minimal change is important because all change causes costs. Some of the costs of change are direct, especially the investments required by the customer. But many other customer costs remain hidden as indirects. They include the costs of retraining and relearning, start-up downtime, error, confusion, and disruption, all of which combine to reduce a customer's productivity and prejudice his product's quality. If you want to minimize a customer's indirect costs, there is no substitute for a superior training program. It must be a featured part of every proposal you make, because of its capability to condense up-front investment time and bring the advantages of your solutions to realization quickly and surely.

Maximum gain is just as important as minimal cost because it certifies the productivity of each dollar of the customer's investment. It is the positive side of the proposal, inducing satisfaction, whereas minimizing customer cost affects the negative side by preventing or limiting dissatisfaction.

Many suppliers think of their proposals as a nuisance, a pro forma requirement to be over and done with as expeditiously as possible so that the real negotiation that determines their sales can begin. This comes from the experience of their vendor heritage where the bidding process serves primarily to set up price negotiations. But your satisfaction proposals will not just get you into the ball game; they *are* the ball game. If you are the winning proposal maker you will be the likeliest winner of the sale.

Proposals are the battlegrounds over which competitions for customer satisfaction are fought. They are the last stop before implementation. Your proposals must, for this reason, work. A customer's operating performance must be improved. So must his financial performance. His rate of return must be satisfactory. So must his value-to-price relationship. All these things must take place within the proposal before a customer can safely permit them to occur within his organization or life style. Any failure beyond the point where the proposal is accepted can have catastrophic consequences for you and your customer alike. It will be too late for either of you to say "I'm sorry."

A failed implementation in a customer's operation can slow him up or shut him down. The direct cost will have been misspent but is probably recoverable. The opportunity cost of his unshipped goods, uncollected receivables, and unattained market share can be devastating. On your part, failed implementation can destroy your repute as a satisfier. You may lose the customer that you have failed, along with the loss of prospective customers who receive, in effect, a negative case history of your work. Worst of all, you stand to lose the opportunity to prove your norms once again, even to improve them, with an additional case history of achievement.

5

Self-Satisfaction and Customer Satisfaction

Once you accept customer satisfaction as your ultimate product, you must learn to be satisfied with yourself only when you have satisfied your customers. Your pride in your products, pride in your processes, and pride in your people must originate from pride in their ability to maximize customer satisfaction. Your appreciation of how good you are must depend on how satisfied your customers are with you. This is the only true measurement of your worth. It will chasten you and force change on you. But it will market-orient you as nothing else can.

As a result, you will be able to see your core customers in a new role. You will see them as your natural allies instead of adversaries who, along with you, share a common interest in adding values to certain activities and operations that both of you depend on for your life styles or livelihoods. In order to improve the quality of their lives or their businesses, your core customers must improve the very things in which you are expert in enhancing. The best way for you to meet your common needs is to partner together rather than increase your costs and dilute your energies and resources in endless bazaar-like haggling over price. It is *value* on which you must focus; the customer's current value, the added value of your norms, and how you can enhance your customers by the addition of your values. These are the only things worth negotiating because these are the only things that are the common denominators for making you and your customers more profitable.

The Core of Corporate Culture

Your core customers must become the core of your corporate culture. For many businesses, this will represent a 180-degree difference from where they are now coming from. Companies whose managers worship at the shrine of their technology, who look inward to what goes into their products instead of looking outward to what values come out of them, will find customer satisfaction to be counter-cultural. So will companies that are organized along matrix lines, where there is no central authority or responsibility for customer satisfaction. Commodity suppliers will need to make significant alterations in how they regard their markets to overcome their habit of thinking of customers as the last stage in their manufacturing and sales processes rather than as the first stage. They will also have to overcome their ingrained belief, fostered by their experience, that it is price and price alone that causes a customer to be satisfied.

Most businesses have a lot to learn about customer satisfaction. First, though, they will have to learn about their customers. Compared to what customers know about their needs and what is required to satisfy them, suppliers tend to know very little. Accordingly, suppliers deal from the only vantage points that they know well: *our company, our products and processes*, and *our competitors*. All the while, their customers are concerned about *their company or family, their products and processes or activities*, and *their competitors*. Suppliers think that they are talking to their customers when they use "our-speak" but, in reality, they are talking *to* themselves *about* themselves. Not only is their communication process faulty, so is its content. If their relationships are not very satisfying to either of them, it is largely because they are not relating.

An inward-looking corporate culture encourages its managers to share with customers all the things that managers do to satisfy themselves: How satisfying their own policies and practices are in reducing their own costs or increasing their own productivity and revenues. Managers in such companies are rarely able to translate their self-satisfaction into meaningful directions for their customers who, by their own perceptions, are different.

"Let us tell you," inner-directed managers say, "How we are looking at the 1990s in terms of forecasting and inventory control or computer-aided design or supermarket shelf display or temporary personnel. Here are our own practices in these areas. And here are our results: Look how low we have reduced our inventory carrying costs; see the increases in store traffic we have created with our new displays."

If customer satisfaction rather than self-satisfaction is the objective, a more conducive theme for sharing values would be "How You Should Be Looking at the 1990s: Competitive Advantages from Inventory Management in Your Industry."

There is no escaping the fact that you must satisfy your customers first if you are to have a satisfactory business. Your own satisfaction is derivative, derived wholly from the satisfaction of your customers. The values you deliver to them must be your transcendent preoccupation. You must satisfy yourself that they are. You must also satisfy your customers. This will require you to price your values so that your customers can see the return you yield on them to be the most satisfying purchase of all—a *bargain* whose high value exceeds even its high price.

When you tap into the mind sets of the managers who run your business, you should find an almost hypnotic focus on relating your value to your price. How, they should be asking themselves all the time, can we maximize customer value? Their answers will become the strategies you will need to maximize your price. That will provide you with the best opportunity you will ever have to combine your own self-satisfaction with customer satisfaction.

Satisfaction and Loyalty

In the same way that customer satisfaction is the key to your profits, customer loyalty is the key to the continuity of satisfaction. Discontinuous satisfaction—working hard to create it, slacking off and losing it, then working even harder to regain it—is cost-ineffective. Only continuity, with its built-in momentum that requires operating at a steady state rather than at superbursts of investment of time and funds, is cost-justifiable. And only a loyal market will support continuity. But what is loyalty?

It is important to understand what loyalty is not before defining loyalty in terms of what it is. Customers are not loyal to products. In this regard, they are similar to their suppliers who think of products as simply today's best trade-off of investments for profits. Nor are customers loyal to suppliers. Today's pheasant can quickly become tomorrow's feather duster.

Customers are loyal solely and exclusively to *value.* Loyalty, then, can be defined as the customer's commitment to optimize his value. Customers are loyal to the maximum value that is available to them; in other words, to the standard of value in their industry. The industry standard-bearer becomes their prime satisfier.

"Loyalty to the greatest satisfaction" is the only safe customer guideline a business can follow. This will drive its managers to understand their customers and cooperate with them in their search for maximum satisfaction. It will also discourage fighting with customers to deny or substitute for their satisfactions. The guideline of greatest satisfaction will radically alter the substance, the time and the cost invested in the sales cycle, freeing it from *unselling*—trying to convince customers that their "must lists" are unnecessary, outmoded, or replaceable.

Unselling is largely unproductive. Often it is counterproductive when it appears to be demeaning to a customer's values. Even when unselling works, it absorbs great amounts of time whose costs can nullify the profits that may eventually be earned. Selling as a loyal supporter of customer values is always easier, significantly more profitable, and invariably a better long-range platform for continued business partnerships.

There are three types of satisfaction values that can command customer loyalty.

1. *The amalgamation of composite values that customers call product quality.* This is not so much based on the values that you put into a product as on the values that your customers can derive from it. It is less the values added by your manufacturing than it is the values added by your application. Quality is the composite of many attributes. They can be construction attributes, performance attributes, or sensory attributes. Whatever they are, their most important aspect is the contribution they make to the quality of their user.

2. *Being a good company to do business with.* This means a company whose guiding sensitivity is to customer satisfaction. To be considered fair and equitable, a company must play square *with the customer*. To be considered prompt and efficient, it must be reliable *with the customer*. To be considered ethical, it must do right *by the customer*. A company must be easy to deal with, which means that it must deal *with the customer* in the ways that he likes to deal and not force or cajole him to deal in terms that are foreign or anathema.

In every industry, there are companies that are good to do business with and others that are not. In some industries, there is a third classification: companies that are "good *not* to do business with." This is an inferred classification, arrived at by logic. These companies are thought of as being good organizations to work for. They make good products. They have good people, good policies, good ethics, and good reputations. But they do not have good market share. When they sell, they must discount. They are not dominant factors anywhere. Their markets have decided that they are good companies *not* to do business with.

The reason why a good company can be a good company not to do business with is invariably the same. It knows its business far better than it knows the businesses of its customers and what will satisfy them the most. The answer is never found in good products or good prices. It is found in good results in the customer's terms.

3. *The value-to-price relationship, the comparison of the value of what is returned to the customer in exchange for the price of his investment required to obtain it.* The third type of value is the most important. Loyalty is always to the value that most exceeds its price. The greater the margin of value over price, the greater the price can be and the greater the loyalty.

The loyalty of a customer is his allegiance to the values that yield him satisfaction. It is difficult to earn, easy to lose, and, if lost, even more difficult to regain. It is not yours to demand. It is, in the manner of an endowment, the customer's privilege to give. You hold it in a temporary trust that is always revocable. The sole guarantee you have is to be the best satisfier. If you remain loyal to that dedication, you have the best chance of having your customer remain loyal to you.

Perceptions of Superior Value

What is marketing if it is not the act of creating perceptions of superior value? These perceptions, not products, are the reasons why customers do business. When a transaction is contemplated, customers ask themselves, what kind of an impact will it make on my business? Will I be improved—if so, by how much and when? If I am asked whether or not I am satisfied, these are the dollar and time values I will refer to for my answer. But in order to do business in the first place, I must perceive that these values will flow to me.

If you have established these values in your name, you have been marketing. If you have not, you have been incurring an unanswered cost no matter what you have called it. Whatever you have been doing, it has not been marketing.

Superior values are the stuff of which superior marketing is made. They are the essence of marketing strategy, which can then simply "tell it like it is." The fewer superior values there are, the greater the reliance that will have to be placed on subterfuge. A revealing way to tell how valuable you are as a satisfier is to clock the amount of time you spend on "marketing strategy." The more time you spend, the likelier it is that you can claim few superior values.

You may be resistant to detecting subterfuge. Your customers, however, will not. They talk straight about satisfaction. They know it when they have it and they know it when they lack it. You cannot tell them what *should* satisfy them or what *must* satisfy them; nor can you successfully redefine the measurements they use. As marketers, you can only serve them with what *does* satisfy them.

Superior marketing is no substitute for superior values. It is a better vehicle for them and it will augment their delivery. Customers can be persuaded to consume your marketing, but it is not what they buy. If you indulge yourself in the superior marketing of inferior values, you will speed their unmasking. In contrast to the superior perceptions that their marketing has aroused, they will appear vapid and wan. On the other hand, adequate marketing of superior values will assure their propagation. This is the optimal recipe for satisfaction, both your own and the satisfaction your customers have in doing business with you.

Superior marketers know this. That is why, like merchandiser L. L. Bean, they guarantee the satisfaction of their customers. In 1912, founder Bean made the commitment to satisfaction that still stands: "I do not consider a sale complete until goods are worn out and the customer is still satisfied." In short, the customer has no alternative.

Appendix A

Satisfying Future Demand Based on Emergent Market Needs

Future prospects are born; future customers are made. They come about as the result of a process to identify them and their needs for satisfaction that flow from the attitude and activity patterns of their daily lives. The needs within these patterns, or life styles, can be used to generate high-satisfaction products and services that match their markets from inception.

There are six common consumer patterns that promise to offer continuing opportunities for satisfaction:

1. Personal care
2. Family business
3. Home economics
4. Travel and entertainment

5. Training and education
6. Environmental management

Personal Care

Supportive Sociotechnological Opportunities and Preclusive Risks

Health care opportunities. Increasing public acceptance of health care as a natural right, and a resultant increase in degree and level of public and private involvement in health care and education. Inadequacy and cost-ineffectiveness of existing professional care system will require deemphasis of MD and hospital as care centers and will encourage deprofessionalization of care to the in-home level. New emphasis on early diagnosis, prevention, and therapy rather than remedial treatment or curative products and services. Growing acceptance of drug values of foods. Increased awareness of health values of psychic experiences.

Health care risks. Governmental and professional medical community resistance to "paramedicalization," deprofessionalization, and other key aspects of therapeutic self-diagnosis and commercially sponsored therapy. High educational input required with both homemaker and professional communities.

Beauty and grooming care opportunities. Multiplied opportunities arising from increasing social correlation of health and beauty, leading to systems potential between foods and cosmetics, beauty and exercise or entertainment, beauty and fashionable apparel and accessories, and the union of psychic and physical health. Emphasis on self-styled care systems which stress individualized beauty. Involvement of the entire family (rather than just the woman) in beauty and grooming. Involvement of the entire body in beauty and grooming, with beauty conceived of as the body's outermost garment of clothing.

Beauty care risks. Saturation of existing distribution systems and difficulty in establishing profitable alternatives. Difficulties of marketing coordinated product systems in a traditionally individual-item business. Increasing governmental sensitivities to drug implications of health-oriented cosmetics. Limiting effects of stepped-up consumerism on beauty care advertising and promotional positioning. Beauty business is style-intensive, stressing high risk over short, faddish product life cycles for potential high reward.

Comments. Health care management is a genuinely new business which has never existed before. As such, it offers attractive opportunities across a wide variety of corporate technological bases. No company has a preemptive manufacturing or marketing foundation. The so-called health care industry, which is really a sick care industry, may enjoy some slight initial advantage, especially in terms of acceptance by the professional medical community. But to the extent that sick care companies are treatment-oriented instead of prevention-oriented, and to the degree that health care can become deprofessionalized and popularized, this advantage may be only transient.

Family Business

Supportive Sociotechnological Opportunities and Preclusive Risks

Opportunities. Increasing feasibility of in-home access to computerized information and data processing services in family business management as a convenience item. Heightened potential of cashless society aspects occurring during the decade of the 1990s. Greater need to systematize multiple family investment options. Growing need for multiple hedges against enduring inflationary dollar erosion. Inexperienced affluence leads to needs for money management advisory and planning services. Rise of interest in consumerism leads to need for increased purchase, label, and packaging information services. Enduring discrepancy between ages of death of husband and wife may lead to need for generalized estate planning services for homemakers. Opportunity to integrate with family dietitian life style and establish purchasing-agent-for-food money management services.

Risks. High educational investment may be required to transform an individualistic, cottage-industry activity into an acceptable commerical function. Potentially high resistance to invasion of fiscal privacy by perceived "Big Brother" image of business management information collection and disbursement services. Technologically intensive and service-intensive business.

Comments. Family business management is an area of profit potential through the 1990s. Taken at its fullest, family business management is a processing business based on computerized data manipulation as its fundamental process. The process is essentially resolved into an investment planning service, with the word "investment" used in its broadest possible context to include all allocations of family economic resources. In this sense, family business management will become more important as affluence increases investment options and inflation reduces the prospective value of each decision.

Home Economics

Supportive Sociotechnological Opportunities and Preclusive Risks

Opportunities. New emphasis on nutrition, functional and health foods, natural foods, and food purity. Technical feasibility of computerized meal planning, supermarket-showroom, and telephone food ordering and delivery sys-

tems. Increasing technical feasibility and social acceptance of food analogs. Acceptance of special-purpose foods
such as body-growth foods, mind-keening foods, beauty
foods, age-retarding and life-extending foods. Disposable
food cooking, serving, and storing systems. Individualized
servings and portion-calorie-controlled foods. Acceptance
of multiple light meal-ettes to replace traditional three
sit-down square meals per day.

Risks. Shorter life cycles for food products. Prospects
for advertising media and supermarket distribution saturation in the face of new food product proliferation. Speculative positioning stance toward food analogs by regula-
tory and distribution agencies as imitations, substitutes,
or new foods. Potentially lessening role emphasis of food-
oriented attitudes and activities in the face of women's
new freedoms and outside concerns.

Comments. Although the regularity of the homemaker's
need to feed and nourish her family as home economics
manager will probably not decrease perceptibly during
the 1990s, the relative importance of the homemaker's
role as foodmaker may decline in her overall role-mix. The
very opportunities which make home economics management profitably rewarding may accelerate the lessening of
its opportunity. First, as food-related attitudes and activities become more and more convenient, homemaker involvement may diminish. Even benign conspiracies such
as "adding the egg" may no longer suffice to simulate
participation. Second, the automation of food ordering,
menu planning, and payment will probably reduce the
onerous and truly time-consuming aspects of some of the
most typical home economics processes. Third, the 1990s'
generation of homemakers may well rebel against kitchen-
centered life styles and food orientation in favor of more
external, more liberated, and more self-expressive roles.

For these reasons, home economics management may
well be a role in downward transition during the 1990s.
The greatest risk lies in *not* pioneering. Two innovative
directions seem most promising of reward. One is the
functionalization of foods, emphasizing their nutrition

and health orientation as if they were delicious drugs; the second is the acknowledgment of the net result of technological developments in food distribution, shopping, and purchase planning, along with an increasing homemaker need for convenience and preplanning and a rising attitude of concern toward the family dietitian role.

Travel and Entertainment

Supportive Sociotechnological Opportunities and Preclusive Risks

Opportunities. Greater mobility and sense of worldliness predispose to wide-ranging travel acceptance. Travel is becoming more informal and periodic and is taking on many attributes of an impulse purchase. Traditional annual vacation is fractionalizing into multiple "vacationettes." Heightened acceptance of rental and disposable vacation products and accessories. Growing guest diversity of in-home entertainment gatherings, including multiracial and multi-lifestyle gatherings. Greater emphasis on cause-oriented socializing and entertainment. More leisure-time and discretionary options for its use through travel and entertainment, leading to enhanced equipment and educational opportunities for athletic, hobby, camping, and allied activities. Increasing acceptance of rent-a-party services. Correlations with snack and disposables development, training and education and family business management life-styles.

Risks. Domestic and international unrest may preclude travel interest and opportunities. Environmental deterioration may also act as discouraging or limiting factor.

Comments. Travel and entertainment will increasingly become intertwined throughout the 1990s. As the commercialization of leisure proceeds, travel will become more convenient, affordable, and acceptable, and will undoubtedly rank high among beneficial forms of entertainment and education. Entertainment, on the other hand, will become more mobile, more portable, and more continuous as an environment which surrounds the individual at almost all times. The ever-present portable radio and in-flight motion pictures are examples of traveling entertainment or of entertaining travel. The net result of the stepped-up melding of travel and entertainment plus education ought to be a market for benefit systems of infinite variety, composed with essential simplicity in their individual modules yet subject to highly complex combinations and permutations depending on personal preference and needs as dictated by the changing variables of time and place.

Training and Education

Supportive Sociotechnological Opportunities and Preclusive Risks

Opportunities. Heightened interest in a wide range of educational activities through in-home and outside-home services: in-home multimedia audiovisual learning systems, study centers, and teaching machines, as well as outside computerized libraries and local learning centers. Greater availability of correspondence study programs and courses in a broad spectrum of subject areas. Educational emphasis placed on vacations, leisure-time activities, social activities, and work, and on self-adjustment, self-selection of knowledge areas, and individual growth. Growing acceptance of behavioral sensitivity training and psychosocial acculturation as normal parts of general education. Greater acceptance of educational toys, games, crafts, and foods. Correlations with travel, entertainment, and all other life styles.

Risks. Unstable market over the short term because of

inevitable shakeout and consolidation of currently over-populated knowledge industry. Failure of technology to regularize second-generation teaching machine perform-ance. Critical sellers' market in educational software.

Comments. Training and educational management is actually two roles with the same name. First, it is a role in itself, with the homemaker acting in ways that develop the intellectual and behavioral capabilities of the family as a group and of its individual members. Second, it is an implicit component of every other lifestyle role which the homemaker plays. As a role itself, training and education has so far been an unstable industry—its hardware capa-bility has eclipsed its software content. The language of systems has been used to disguise the absence of a true systematization in either manufacturing or marketing. On the basis of this background, it is difficult to assess the next decade of development of the education business or so-called knowledge industry. It is easier to foresee an opportunity of clearer magnitude for training and educa-tion management activities as adjuncts to all the other major life roles. This suggests that an information module be considered an integral characteristic of every major product and service system. It also encourages the wisdom of conceiving of information sources as profit-making cor-porate media, instead of regarding only products as me-dia, and establishing those information media as the ma-jor creators of market preference for the products which may, in a subordinate or supplementary role, accompany them.

Environmental Management

Supportive Sociotechnological Opportunities and Preclusive Risks

Internal environmental opportunities. Greater interest in environmental coordination of furnishings, appliances, and accessories by means of systems. Increasing acceptance by women of "man of the house" role, opening new decision-making opportunities and product options. Increasing acceptance of rental as opposed to purchase options and of disposable options as opposed to permanent possession. New concepts and materials proliferation, including plastics and other synthetics, inflatables, foldables, storables, multiple-purpose units, and portables. Greater needs for emergency, security, and safety products and services in the face of increasing crime and social unrest. Increased desire for privacy and individualization of internal environment. Heightened acceptance of interior environment as education-entertainment-information center for family. Potential correlation with food systems engineering to create programmed home cooking center as environmental focal point. Potential correlation of home business management center with family business management lifestyle role of money handling.

Internal environment risks. Rapid product obsolescence. Increasing competition from out-of-home discretionary investments. Dependence on appliance-service orientation and appliance-type distribution system. Involvement is complicated by interrelationships between electronics technology, plumbing, heating, electricity, fixtures, home construction codes, and labor union restrictions.

External environment opportunities. Greater acceptance of external environment as extension of indoors (the lawn as carpeting, the auto as a portable room). Increasing acceptance of rental as opposed to purchase options and of disposable options as opposed to permanent possession. New concepts and new materials, including plastics and other synthetics, foldables and storables, prefabricated and modular units. Range of external environment expanded by means of house trailers and houseboats (which make a second homesite available almost anywhere), ski houses, summer houses, and other types of second homes. Greater needs for property value insurance and security and safety products and services because of increasing crime and social unrest. Correlations with training, education, travel, and entertainment.

External environment risks. Rapid product obsolescence. External environmental deterioration and resulting governmental regulation may limit extension and discourage involvement or investment.

Comments. Environmental management, both internal and external, is not a truly new business even though it may seem to be. Instead, it is largely a new systematization of many heretofore individual businesses which have recently positioned themselves in alliance with each other. Time-space and geographical space are now equally regarded as environments, and there can be a high degree of potential profitability in seeking to fill them since each is more encompassing than ever before.

Appendix B

Satisfying Future Demand Based on Emergent Growth Technologies

The development of products that satisfy is too important, to say nothing of being too expensive, to be left to chance. The "something-will-turn-up school" is closed. In its place, a process exists to improve the probability of coming up with highly satisfying new products on a planned, predictable basis. The process depends on three capabilities:

1. Access to emergent developmental technologies that can serve as the capability bases of highly profitable new businesses.
2. Knowledge of high-added-value market applications for these technologies.
3. A method for validating and ranking the most prof-

itable business concepts linking the technologies to their market applications.

The process consists of six steps: (1) discovery, (2) data basing, (3) Delphi testing, (4) distillation, (5) due diligence, and (6) decision making.

Objectives of the Product-Development Process

Each time this process is cycled, it has two objectives. One is to achieve a hit ratio of one winner from every eight candidates. The other is a survival-to-loss ratio of three profit-making survivors for every two whose profits are lost to break-even or failure.

The 1-in-8 Hit Ratio

In order to be cost-effective, the minimum yield of a growth cycle must be at least one valid Big Winner from every batch of eight alleged Big Winners. This will enable growth to be fairly predictable, reasonably consistent, and largely self-financing through the recycling of profits. It will also allow growth to become familiar, making it the rule rather than an exception. If the yield of Big Winners is stretched thinner than one in eight, growth becomes chancy and sporadic; it loses it rhythm as a planned, periodic event and may never be able to catch up paying back its development costs from profits.

Out of every cycle's eight growth candidates, each an alleged Big Winner, a maximum of three can safely be lost between the time the refinement process starts and the final cut begins. Of the five survivors left, the most likely result, which is shown in Figure 9, is as follows:

- One Big Winner, a new business with a minimum 30 percent annual rate of growth over its first three years

FIGURE 9.   THE 1-IN-8 HIT RATIO.

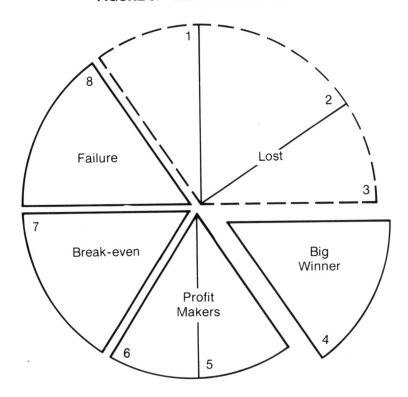

and a minimum annual gross revenue of $25 million by the third year.

- Two profit makers, new businesses with lower annual rates of growth and a smaller annual gross revenue contribution.
- One break-even business, a new business that pays back its investment without contributing a positive return.
- One failure, a new business that does not achieve break-even by the third year.

This outcome can be looked at as if it were a statement of sources and distribution of growth funds. The Big Winner and the two profit makers are the profit sources for each growth cycle. The Big Winner's funds are the prime source of expanded corporate earnings. The new income from the two profit makers pays for the cycle's investment, allowing it to be internally financed. The two remaining businesses, the break-even and the failure, are costs. The break-even business is an opportunity cost. The failure is a direct cost.

The 3-to-2 Survival-to-Loss Ratio

At each phase of a growth cycle, refinement takes place. When the cycle begins, all the candidates look good. On a judgemental basis, it is often hard to choose between them; all eight may look like Big Winners, thereby encouraging a euphoric "bonanza psychology" among management that will swiftly be disabused at the cycle's first turn.

After the cycle's first phase of concept testing and screening, six of the original eight growth candidates will probably survive and two will be lost. After the second phase, market testing, five of the surviving six candidates will still be survivors, while one more candidate will be lost. Finally, after commercialization, three of the five candidates will be money makers and the other two will be losers. Of the three money makers, one can be the Big Winner. Figure 10 shows the entire process, with the 3-to-2 ratio illustrated in the third phase of the cycle.

This survival-to-loss experience acts like a probability curve to dictate the need for cranking up each growth cycle with eight prime candidates. No lesser number will yield the requisite three money makers. Nothing less than truly prime candidates will survive the winnowing process to yield the one Big Winner. Unless there is a continuing supply of premier business opportunities to put into the hopper, management will be unable to count on producing a Big Winner from each development cycle. As either the quantity of candidates diminishes or their quality decreases, the odds against winners rise automatically.

FIGURE 10.   THE 3-TO-2 SURVIVAL-TO-LOSS RATIO.

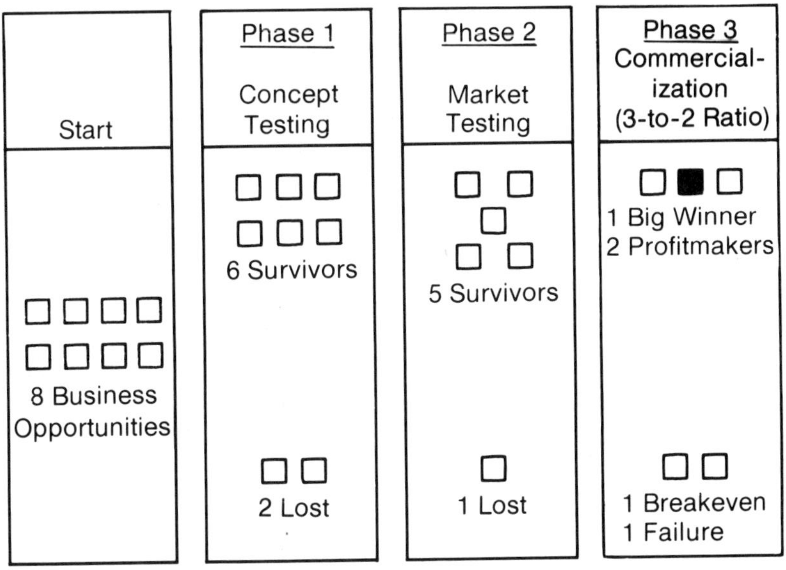

Start	Phase 1 Concept Testing	Phase 2 Market Testing	Phase 3 Commercial- ization (3-to-2 Ratio)
☐ ☐ ☐ ☐ ☐ ☐ ☐ ☐ 8 Business Opportunities	☐ ☐ ☐ ☐ ☐ ☐ 6 Survivors	☐ ☐ ☐ ☐ ☐ 5 Survivors	☐ ■ ☐ 1 Big Winner 2 Profitmakers
	☐ ☐ 2 Lost	☐ 1 Lost	☐ ☐ 1 Breakeven 1 Failure

Steps in the Product–Development Process

If management's criteria make sense for growth and if its capabilities and commitment are strong, the six phases of the Big Winner development process take place. It is shown in Figure 11. The culmination of the process is a business case, from which a market-penetration plan can be drawn.

Phase 1. Discovery

The discovery of new business opportunities based on emergent technologies takes two forms: an internal search for opportunities that can be generated by corporate technologies, and an external search of opportunities from a global brainbank.

FIGURE 11.   THE BIG WINNER PROCESS.

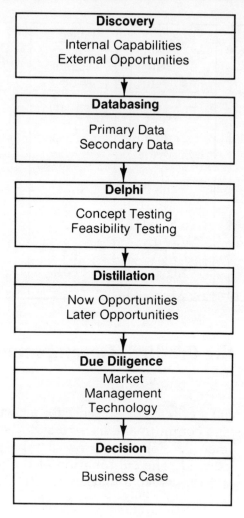

Internally, two things should be looked for. The first is the potential to migrate a mainstream science into growth areas. The second is the existence of a renegade technology hiding out among the bunsen burners and breadboards, being pursued as a zealous vigil by a single individual or a hardy band during lunch hours, evenings and weekends. From these scientists-in-hiding can come the deviations from corporate mainstreams that lead to winning commercializations.

On a external, global basis a brainbank must be formed of leading doers, thinkers, and devil's advocates in emergent technologies and their market applications. Typical brainbanks include inventors, scientists, incipient entrepreneurs in pre-corporate business groups, business analysts, government agency experts, business, trade, and professional association leaders, consultants, venture capital and other financial sources for new technology-based businesses, and industry-watchers in the United States, Western Europe, and the Pacific Basin countries.

The function of the brainbank is to act as the authoritative source of primary data on their technologies. They are the horse's mouth; from them can be learned all that is knowable. What is a new science composed of? What other technologies does it draw from? What are its most likely migrations? What other technologies complement it or compete with it? What are its principal commercial applications—with what market segments, yielding what benefits to meet what needs at what probable value-to-price ratios? When will it be marketable? Who are its best developers; its best managers; its heaviest sponsors?

Phase 2. Data Basing

Through personal interviews, mail, and telephone, the brainbank's knowledge, activities, and opinions are collated into a data base on emergent technologies that are relevant to corporate growth objectives. These data are supplemented with secondary information from a global search of publicly available sources from individuals, institutions, and government publications and libraries.

The data base may be thought of as a central repository of the raw materials from which future business can be made. Once amassed, they must be fashioned into business concepts: beneficial values that are expressed as if they were already deliverable—prepositioning statements for potential businesses.

An example model concept statement would read as follows:

> Batch production of customized products as small as single units can now be cost-effectively manufactured, even in between mass-production runs. Switchover and switch-back can be automatically accomplished within 100 nano-seconds, reducing downtime for all practical purposes to zero. Productivity is improved an average of 5 to 7 percent while costs can be reduced up to $10,000 per shift. These results are accomplished by a flexible manufacturing sys-tem (FMS) that employs computerized robots guided by expert system software. The FMS work stations require maintenance on the average of once every 100,000 hours and need no human attendants to operate, service, or change programs. An FMS of this type can be installed on-line for approximately $100,000 and can return the invest-ment in full within six months.

A concept statement will undergo progressive enhance-ment if it attracts brainbank interest, having value added to it by the inclusion of cost-benefit analyses of operating benefits, bench-test results, advertisements, and eventu-ally in-use tests of prototype systems.

Phase 3. Delphi Testing

Through the serial process of iteration and reiteration known as the Delphi method, business concepts are circu-lated through the brainbank. Delphi requires an ever-narrowing evaluation of each concept: What are its per-ceived assets and liabilities, how do they compare with competitive concepts, what is their relative likelihood of Big Winner commercialization, what is their most proba-ble time frame and most likely market composition? Mar-kets themselves, once they have been identified, can also participate in the Delphi phase. First by relatively broadscale exposure, then by successively more vertical market nicheing, the most likely user segment will be sought. The target will be a user group whose needs are sufficiently met by the business concept's technical capability to yield operating and financial benefits that merit a premium price. Without a sizable group of such users, there can be no Big Winner. Finding several small groups, or groups who perceive only minimal benefits, is no substitute for a single significantly benefitted user cluster. Nor is a propensity to buy cheap, even in volume, a suitable substitute for a premium price.

The classic mistake to be avoided is the one made by IBM for its PCjr. According to IBM itself, the company misjudged who would buy the product. Business managers for whom it was intended found it unsatisfactory in construction and performance. They also found it overpriced. The secondary market of home users reacted in the same way to its price; they were unwilling to pay IBM's premium. The product had no place to go.

Concept statements, concept advertising, and proforma cost–benefit projections allow great flexibility in testing multiple solutions to the same market opportunity. Their downside comes from eliciting hypothetical responses to their patently unreal proposals. Prototype products can bring the real world closer but pay a price in flexibility. They are what they are, warts and all, and they may therefore narrowly focus critique on their specific configuration and performance rather than on the broader concept they are intended to represent.

Phase 4. Distillation

The highest priority business concepts, each representing an emergent technology and its market applications, are ranked in an order of "now opportunities"—business opportunities worthy of immediate involvement through minority investment, joint venturing, or R&D partnering—and "later opportunities," which may require further study and lengthier tracking.

Phase 5. Due Diligence

Each entepreneurial group, whether precorporate or actually in business, that offers a "now opportunity" must be evaluated to determine how partnerable, acquirable, or investible it is. Due diligence should focus on three primary growth factors, key characteristics that have been found to best predict fast profitable growth: *management*, in terms of its personal and professional background, leadership in technical skills, and commitment to growth; *market*, in terms of its projectable growth potential; and *technology*, in terms of its leading-edge nature, time and dollar costs of commercialization, comparative cost-effectiveness, barriers and constraints to life-cycle growth, predictable obsolescence rate, and derivative technologies and applications.

Phase 6. Decision Making

A business case can now be prepared on each emergent opportunity. It will serve as the platform for a growth plan. The case states the facts about a business. It defines its technology base, market segmentation, product lines and their value-to-price relationships, and competitive and economic influencing factors. A business case discusses criteria for entry, such as richness, readiness, and reasonableness in relationship to business fit. A plan based on it will be able to calculate the growth that can be brought to the case and the preferred method for acquiring the opportunity.

Problems to Anticipate

Fit vs. Future

A primary criterion for growth with most mature businesses is fit. For such businesses, a logical connection must exist between existing products and anything new. More often than not, this means that the technology must be familiar. A chemicals processor, for example, sees a fit with hydrocarbon processing while electronic data processing is viewed as an alien science. Almost every *Fortune* 500 company can show scars that prove the validity of sticking to one's own knitting as far as growth is concerned. During the diversification craze of the 1970s, technology fit was subordinated as a growth standard for considerations of counter-cyclical cash flow or quick speculative return. Because there was no inherent glue to bind disparate business—and because it was discovered that there is no such animal as "a good manager who can manage anything"—the frenzy to diversify has led directly to a much less-well-publicized frenzy to divest.

No one is anxious to repeat this process, which is costly in resources, repute, and human suffering. As a result, top management frequently asks for four to six new businesses, over a five to seven year time frame, that "fit within the realm" of the current business. Giant steps, no matter how inviting, are discouraged even when they can be taken with minimal risk. Instead, management lets it be known that growth begins—and ends—"a half-step removed" from where the business is perceived to be today. This is the time-honored way by which commodities-based mature businesses produce commodities-based new businesses.

Taking half-steps to growth is a necessary component of a comprehensive growth process. It enables a business to keep up with the natural evolution of its technologies and the changes in its markets' segmentation. Linked to the sponsorship of internal venturers who come to management for funds to commercialize their own ideas, logical extension helps make sure that the asset base of the business, already bought and paid for, is being fully capitalized and insured against opportunity loss. But fit-based strategies have one other factor in common as well. Neither separately nor together are they likely to produce a true Big Winner business for the future.

Today's corporate realm is yesterday's future, not to-morrow's. While it is demonstrably possible to develop a handful of close-fit business that will cumulatively yield after-tax earnings of $50 million by year five or seven, it is almost impossible to produce one business that will make such a contribution by itself or, in the manner of a Big Winner, exceed it. This is the difference between going for the home run and going for singles. While it is true that a series of singles can equal a home run, and that they are presumably easier to make, the home runs are largely concentrated in the emergent businesses of the future. This is home run country. If management wants to be a leader of the future, there is no substitute for swinging for the fences.

By definition, growth into emergent technologies can-not fit within today's existing realm. This is its proof of being emergent. Some companies abide by a rule of thumb that warns, "If it fits, it's probably already ma-ture." They base their thinking on the belief that busi-nesses, like people, pass along a genetic inheritance to their offspring. Some of the deterministic code may be technological: A science may have lost its ability to com-mercialize products at Big Winner margins. Other codes may be connected to the market. A market may be declin-ing in size, altering its propensity to purchase, or using only price as its buying guide. Representing half-steps from their parent business, offspring with their same heredity are generally preordained to replicate their par-ents' competitiveness for margins and market share with the same unspectacular results that encouraged their con-ception in the first place.

Eight-Barrel Pumpers

The ability to come up consistently with one Big Winner out of every eight new business opportunities depends on three factors:

1. A process for creating a continuing supply of high-quality opportunities to feed into the wide end of the hopper.
2. A process for testing the likelihood of each opportunity as a potential Big Winner profit producer.
3. A corps of trained entrepreneurial managers who can realize the full profit of each Big Winner opportunity.

Success starts at the top. The productivity of the testing process and the impact of the entrepreneurial managers clearly depend on the opportunities that are presented for testing and, if they survive, for management. There must be enough of them. They must each possess above-average intrinsic values. Unless their supply can be ensured, mediocrity will become inherent in corporate development. New business will be developed, but it will overwhelmingly be what the oil industry calls "eight barrel pumpers": marginal profit makers that cannot be dismissed as dry holes yet never fulfill the expectation that someday they will become gushers.

Eight-barrel pumpers are the bane of corporate development. They clog the system, require the investment of irreplaceable management resources without commensurate return, and prevent the pursuit of true Big Winners. Their opportunity cost is incalculable. Even after mediocrity has become obvious, each is protected by an advocacy that acts to postpone its disposition. Meanwhile, the euphoria of seeming to grow multiple new businesses deceives top management into complacency about its readiness for the future.

No major company requires, or can cope with, a large number of marginally profitable development businesses. A system that generates them is riddled with cost-ineffectiveness from its inception. Yet many corporations invite this very result. They operate without a method explicity designed to deliver Big Winners. Instead, they solicit broadscale ideas from their own people, funding them almost randomly, or they spin out internal support services into free-standing subsidiary businesses. These models can be useful supplements to a Big Winner growth strategy. But wholesale dependence on them only assures the appearance of growth without its substance.

Half-Stepping

To stop short of reaching out to the emergent sciences is to truncate the development process by limiting it to the markets and sciences of yesterday and today. What is considered to be "new" by a developing company may be the long-established domain of competitors. Simply introducing an innovation as "the new kid on the block" earns little or nothing. Only by breaking out into yet-uncompetitive arenas where ingenuity and insight are key determinants of success and where markets are up for grabs can the constraints imposed by maturity on premium margins be overcome.

In order to be a prominent player in the arena of emergent technologies, development managers must understand their unique role in the growth process. While most companies could well say, "We're not growing half as well close to home as we know how," growth should not be allowed to become a serial function.

A policy of logical extension by half-steps first, followed by market amplification by full steps, and finally a giant step or two into emergent technologies is an infinite postponement of winning big for the future. It is practically a guarantee that current core businesses will remain the chief corporate dependence, accounting for 80 percent or more of annual profits while new businesses never achieve more than 3 to 5 percent. In sunset industries whose base businesses have long ago lost their thrust as high profit sources, deferring entry into emerging sciences can be fatal if there is nothing to take their place when what du Pont has called "the end of the rainbow" is passed. For industries and businesses that are not yet at sunset, but are lingering where dusk and twilight are deepening, development of emergent technologies may be the best survival strategy. (Other options include scaling down or being bought in a friendly takeover transaction.) But even without these threats, it is urgent to know how the technologies of the future will play a major role in future customer satisfaction.

Index